# LONGMAN

# Elementary Dictionary

# Longman

spelling of the new word

## pack

picture relating to the example

definition

*to put things in a bag or box*

example

Christopher is **packing** his clothes. Tomorrow he is going to America.

## circus

difficult plurals

*plural* **circuses**

You can see a lot of animals and dancers at a **circus**.

## dirty

difficult comparatives and superlatives

**dirtier, dirtiest**
Peter played football this morning. He fell down. Now he is very **dirty**. He must have a wash.

## burst

difficult parts of verbs

**bursting, burst, burst**

*to come open suddenly*
"There are too many things in that bag. It will **burst**!"

## bat

**1** *a small animal with wings*
**Bats** sleep in the day and fly at night.

more than one meaning

**2** We use a **bat** when we hit a ball.

## blow

**blowing, blew, blown**

**1** The wind **blew** all day yesterday. My hat **blew** off my head.

**2** The wind **blew** my hat off my head.

more than one way of using a word

Nick **blew** the butterfly off his hand.

## carry

**carries, carrying, carried, carried**

**1** Tom is **carrying** some books.

**2 to carry on**
*to continue*
The lesson ended, but Kate **carried on** reading her book. She read her book until the start of the next lesson.

phrasal verbs

## fed

**1** *past and part of* **feed**
Nick **fed** the horse this morning.
It doesn't need food now.

idioms

**2 fed up**
*not happy*
"I don't like working in this
office. I'm **fed up** with this job."

## dry

*adjective* **drier, driest**
**1** The desert is very **dry**. There
is no water there.

*verb* **dries,
drying, dried,
dried**
**2** Peter is
**drying** his
hair.

## drew

*past of* **draw**
Paul **drew** a picture of his
house at school yesterday.

## busier

Yesterday I was very busy, but
today I am even **busier**.

## children

*plural of* **child**
"How old are your **children**,
Jane?" – "Peter is fourteen,
Lisa is thirteen, and Paul is ten."

## don't

*do not*
**1** I like oranges, but I **don't** like
bananas.

**2** "**Don't** play in the road!"

## eye

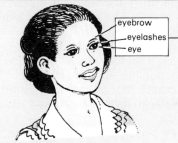

eyebrow
eyelashes
eye

*a part of the face*
We see with our **eyes**.

## exam or examination

*an important test*
At the end of the year we have
our school **exams**.

"Did you pass your English
**exam**?" – "Yes. I got eighty
per cent (80%)."

## bicycle

Peter is on his
**bicycle**.

**Bike** is another
word for
**bicycle**.

## cassette

**1** Helen is holding a **cassette**.
**2 cassette recorder**
Helen is putting a cassette in
the **cassette recorder**.

---

*Margin labels (left column):*

- idioms
- more than one part of speech
- separate entries for difficult parts of verbs
- separate entries for difficult comparatives and superlatives
- separate entries for difficult plurals
- contractions

*Margin labels (right column):*

- labels to make meaning clearer
- alternative forms
- other words with the same meaning
- related words

# Introduction

The **Longman Elementary Dictionary** is a new type of dictionary intended to help students learn English more effectively.

The dictionary contains 2000 important English words which a student needs from the start. English language teaching books have been analysed to ensure that all the most useful English words have been included in the dictionary.

A completely new principle has been used in the **Longman Elementary Dictionary**. The most basic words - those which a student learns first - are defined simply by the use of a clear explanatory example, usually with a picture. This technique shows the use of the word in an easily accessible way, and will be of great benefit to beginners.

There are many other ways in which the **Longman Elementary Dictionary** helps students:

**1** All the definitions and examples are written in very simple language, so that even students working on their own can understand them.

**2** The examples show how English words are used, and so give the students an indication of how to construct natural English sentences.

**3** The illustrations are clear and attractive. They will help the students understand and remember what the word means and the context in which it is used.

**4** The pictures refer directly to the examples, so that the example and the picture together make the meaning as clear as possible.

**5** Difficult plurals and verb parts are shown in full, so students will learn about the grammar of words as well as learning what they mean.

**Longman Group UK Limited,**
Longman House, Burnt Mill, Harlow,
Essex CM20 2JE, England
and Associated Companies throughout the world.

First published 1987
Second impression 1988

Produced by Longman Singapore Publishers (Pte) Ltd.
Printed in Singapore

British Library Cataloguing in Publication Data

Longman elementary dictionary.
  1. English language——Dictionaries
  423          PE1628

ISBN 0-582-96405-9

## A NOTE TO TEACHERS

The **Longman Elementary Dictionary** has been specially written as a first learning dictionary and can be used to help students develop and practise basic dictionary skills.

Here are some suggestions for using the dictionary in class:
**1** You can use the dictionary to practise the order of the English alphabet. For example, you might give your students a list of three or four words beginning with different letters, like **eat**, **ball**, **lemon**, **day**, and ask them to write them down in the correct alphabetical order: **ball**, **day**, **eat**, **lemon**.

**2** If you are teaching a new word, you can ask the students to try to guess the meaning of the word from the context, and then look it up in the dictionary. Get them to read out the definition or examples to reinforce the learning of that particular word. You might then ask them to think of new examples of their own.

**3** Ask your students to open their dictionaries at a page containing a lot of pictures, for example at the page with the word "bag" on it. Without telling them which word you are looking at, describe the picture at "bag" to them in English. ("There is one person in the picture . . . It is a girl . . . She has got short hair . . . She is standing up . . . She is wearing a sweater . . . She is holding something . . .") See who is the first to guess the correct word. Students can perhaps try the exercise for themselves, either in small groups or as a class. Describing the pictures will also help to increase their vocabulary.

**4** Write some sentences on the blackboard, for example:

The sky is always **blue**.
Everyone likes **bright** colours.
The middle of an egg is **yellow**.

Underline the key word in each sentence. Then ask the students, "Are these sentences true or false?" If they do not know the answer, they will have to look up the key word and find out. This is a good way to help your students learn sets of related words: you can do the same for words referring to animals, furniture, fruit, games, measurements, time, parts of the body, occupations, and so on.

COMPILED BY THE LONGMAN ELT REFERENCE DEPARTMENT:

| | |
|---|---|
| *Editorial Director* | Della Summers |
| *Publisher* | Sue Maingay |
| *Editors* | Sue Lambert, Fiona McIntosh |

| | |
|---|---|
| *Illustrators* | John Fraser, Steve Lings (Linden Artists), Clyde Pearson, Mark Peppé |
| *Colouring* | Clyde Pearson |
| *Design* | Malcolm Booker, Geoff Sida (cover), Douglas Williamson |
| *Production* | Clive McKeough |

# A a

## a

1 "Have you got **a** bicycle or **a** car?" – "**A** bicycle."
There is **a** cat on the wall. The cat is black.
2 *for each*
Rice costs fifty pence **a** kilogram.

We use **a** before words that do not begin with a, e, i, o, or u: He saw **a** lion and **a** camel.

We use **an** before words that begin with a, e, i, o, or u, and also before some words that begin with h: He saw **an** elephant.

## able to

I can drive, but I am not **able to** use my car today. The car is at the garage. I will be **able to** use the car tomorrow.

## aboard

*on or into a boat, ship, or plane*
All the people went **aboard** the ship. Then the ship left.

## about

1 Tom is reading a book **about** England.
2 There are **about** eight million people in London.
3 **about to**
The train leaves at three o'clock. Now it is one minute to three. The train is **about to** leave.

## above

The picture of my family is **above** the picture of my father.

## abroad

*to or in a different country*
David is going **abroad** for a holiday this year. He is going to America.

## absent

"Is Alan at school today?" – "No. He is **absent** because he is ill."

## accident

Robert had an **accident**. His car hit a wall. We took him to the hospital.

## across

Helen is walking **across** the road.
"Look at this river. Can you swim **across** to the other side?"

## act

*to be in a play or a film*
Marlon Brando **acts** in films.

## actor

*a man in a play or a film*
Marlon Brando is an **actor**.

## actress

*plural* **actresses**
*a woman in a play or a film*
Elizabeth Taylor is an **actress**.

## add

1 **Add** three and four, and you get seven (3 + 4 = 7).
Three and four **add up to** seven.
2 *to say something else*
"My name's Maria," she said. Then she **added**, "I come from Spain."

## address

*plural* **addresses**
"Where do you live, Simon?" – "I live in London. My **address** is: 23 Princes Street, London."

## adjective

*a word that tells you something about a noun*
"Small", "good", and "happy" are all **adjectives**. That house is *small*. It is a *small* house.

## adult

There are three **adults** and two children in the picture.

## adventure

1 Sindbad went to many places. He had a lot of **adventures**.
2 **adventure park**
In an **adventure park**, there are many things to do. You can

buy nice things to eat, and there are small cars that go round and round very fast.

# adverb

*a word that tells you something about a verb*
"Slowly", "badly", and "happily" are **adverbs**. Robert drives his car *slowly*.

# advertisement

Yesterday Tom saw an **advertisement** for a new drink. Then he went to the shop and bought a bottle of the new drink.

# advice

"Can you give me some **advice**, father?" – "Yes, of course." – "What do you think I should study at university?"

# aeroplane

Lisa flew from Paris to London in an **aeroplane**.
**Plane** is another word for **aeroplane**.

# afraid

A lion came into the village. The people were **afraid**. They were **afraid of** the lion.

# after

Tuesday comes **after** Monday. Tuesday comes before Wednesday.

# afternoon

1 We go to school in the morning. In the **afternoon** we go home.
2 **"Good afternoon."**
When you see someone in the afternoon, you say, **"Good afternoon."**

# afterwards

We went to the cinema and saw the film. **Afterwards** we walked home.

# again

I read this book last year. Now I am reading it **again**.

# against

1 Peter's back is **against** the tree.

2 We played football at school last week. We played **against** a different school.

# age

"What **ages** are your children?" – "Nick is fourteen years old, and Maria is thirteen."

# ago

*in the past*
"When did you see him?" – "I saw him three days **ago**."

# agree

**agreeing, agreed, agreed**
1 *to think the same as someone*
"I think this book is very good." – "I don't **agree** with you. I didn't like it."
2 *to say "yes" to something*
Helen wanted to go to London with Lisa's family. She asked her father if she could go. He **agreed**.

# ahead

*in front*
"I can see a town **ahead**."
Peter and Nick are running. Peter is **ahead of** Nick. Nick is behind Peter.

# air

We live on land. Fish live in the sea. Birds and planes fly in the **air**.

# airline

"Which **airline** did you fly to England with?" – "I flew with British Airways."

# airmail

Letters go from Spain to London by **airmail**. A plane takes the letters.

# airport

You can see many planes at an **airport**.

# alive

*living*
Steven's grandfather is dead, but his grandmother is still **alive**.

# all

1 *every one of*
**All** the children in the school were early today. They were **all** there at eight o'clock. No one was late.
**All of** us like ice cream.
2 **all right**
"Please carry this for me." –

"**All right**. Give it to me."
"How are you?" – I'm **all right**, thank you."

## allow

Alan wanted to see his father in the hospital. The teacher **allowed** him to leave the class.

## almost

"Can you get that apple for me?" – "No. I can **almost** touch it, but it's too high."

## alone

*without other people*
Tom was the only student in the classroom. He was **alone**.

## along

Peter went to the shop. He walked **along** the street, and then he turned right.

## aloud

Maria read the book **aloud** to her young brother. He listened to the story.

## alphabet

The English **alphabet** has twenty-six letters.
This is the English **alphabet**:
a b c d e f g h i j k l m n o p q r s t u v w x y z

## already

"We're going to do this exercise today." – "But we've **already** done it. We did it last week."

## also

Peter plays football very well. He **also** swims very well.

## although

**Although** it was raining, Michael played football.
**Though** is another word for **although**.

## always

Alan gets up at seven o'clock every day. He **always** gets up at seven o'clock.

## am

*part of* **be**
"Are you cold?" – "Yes, **I am**."

## a.m.

*in the morning*
The bus leaves at seven **a.m.** (7.00 **a.m.**).

## among

There are trees around this house. The house is **among** the trees.

## amount

I paid a large **amount** of money for my new car. The car was very expensive.

## an

1 "Do you want **an** apple or **an** ice cream?" – "**An** apple, please."

There is **an** old book on the table. The book is a hundred years old.
**2** *for each*
That car can go at a hundred kilometres **an** hour.

We use **an** before words that begin with a, e, i, o, or u, and also before some words that begin with h: He ate **an** apple and **an** orange.

We use **a** before words that do not begin with a, e, i, o, or u: He ate **a** banana and **a** tomato.

## and

I bought two things in a shop today. I bought a pen **and** some paper.

## anger

Peter broke his sister's camera. His sister was very angry, but she did not show her **anger**.

## angry

**angrier, angriest**
A lorry hit Robert's car. Robert was very **angry**. He shouted at the lorry driver.

## animal

Lions, horses, and dogs are **animals**.

## another

*one more*
"Would you like **another** cup of coffee?" – "Yes, please."

"Though" is **another** word for "although".

## answer

*noun*
**1** "How many people live in London?" – "I know the **answer** to that question. The **answer** is: eight million people."

*verb*
**2** "Can anyone **answer** the question about London?" – "Yes, I can **answer** it. There are eight million people in London."

# ant

*an insect*
**Ants** are black or brown.

# any

"Have you got **any** sugar?" – "No, I'm sorry, I haven't got **any**. But Helen has got some."

# anybody or anyone

"Is there **anybody** in the classroom?" – "No. There's no one at school. Today is a holiday."

# anything

It was very dark. I could not see **anything**.

# anywhere

"Where's my key? I've looked everywhere, but I can't find it **anywhere**."

# appear

*to be seen*
You cannot see the stars in the day. The stars only **appear** at night.

# apple

*a round fruit*
**Apples** are red, yellow, or green.

# apricot

*a round yellow fruit*
**Apricots** grow on trees. They grow in hot places.

# April

*the fourth month of the year*
There are thirty days in **April**.

# are

*part of* **be**
Maria is from Spain. Helen and Kate **are** from England. The boys **are** playing football.

# area

**1** "Is there a school near here?" – "No. There isn't a school in this **area**."
**2** Each side of that field is thirty metres long. The **area** of the field is 900 (30 x 30) square metres (900 m²).

# aren't

*are not*
"Are Nick and Tom brothers?" – "No, they **aren't**."

# arm

*a part of the body*
Peter hurt his **arm** when he was playing football.

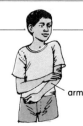
arm

# army

*plural* **armies**
William is a soldier. He is in the **army**.

# around

There is a wall **around** Tom's house. His dog cannot get out.

# arrival

The plane will come to London at six o'clock. The **arrival** time of the plane is six o'clock.

# arrive

**arriving, arrived, arrived**
The plane leaves London at eleven o'clock and **arrives** in Paris at twelve o'clock.

# art

In the **art** lesson we draw pictures.

# artist

*a person who paints or draws pictures*
Picasso was a famous **artist**.

# as

**1** "Is Helen good at English?" – "Yes, but she's not **as** good **as** Susan."
**2** *when, while*
Maria looked in the shop windows **as** she walked along the street.
**3** *because*
I could not see the house, **as** it was very dark.
**4** *the same as*
David and Robert both have blue cars. David's car is **the same** colour **as** Robert's car.
**5** *as well as*
Martin has a car. He has a bicycle, too. He has a bicycle **as well as** a car.

# ask

**1** *to say a question*
"Where do you live?" Jane **asked**.
Jane **asked** the woman where she lived.
**2** *to ask for*
The student said, "Can I have a pen?" She **asked for** a pen.

## asleep

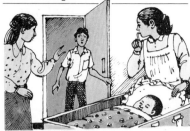

**1** *sleeping*
"Don't make a noise. The baby is **asleep**."
**2 to fall asleep**
*to go to sleep*
Alan **fell asleep** when he was watching television yesterday.

## astronaut

This **astronaut** is walking on the moon.

## at

**1** Helen didn't bring her bag home. The bag is **at** her friend's house.
"Where is Susan?" – "She's **at** school."
**2** Martin left the factory **at** five o'clock today.
**At night** you can see the moon.

## ate

*past of* **eat**
Tom **ate** nine oranges yesterday.

## August

*the eighth month of the year*
There are thirty-one days in **August**.

## aunt

*the sister of your father or your mother*

Robert's mother has two sisters. They are Robert's **aunts**.

## author

*a person who writes a book*
Charles Dickens was an **author**. He wrote many books.
**Writer** is another word for **author**.

## autumn

*a part of the year*
**Autumn** comes after summer and before winter.
In some countries, the leaves fall off the trees in **autumn**.

## average

There are three schools in our town. One school has 250 students, one has 350 students, and one has 600 students. The **average** number of students is 400.
$(250 + 350 + 600 = 1200$
$1200 \div 3 = 400)$

## awake

*not sleeping*
Louise's baby isn't asleep now. He's **awake**.

## away

**1** Mark is walking **away** from the post office. Jenny is walking towards it.
**2** Martin wants to go **away** from his village. He wants to live in a big town.
**3** "Is Steven here?" – "No, he's **away**. He's in France."

## awful

*very bad*
"That book is **awful**!"

# B b

## baby

*plural* **babies**
*a very young child*
Louise has a new **baby**. Louise is the mother of the **baby**.

## back

**1** Peter has his **back** against the tree.

**2** Susan is sitting at the **back** of the classroom. The teacher is at the front.
**3** Susan is sitting in the **back** row of the classroom.
**4** *not forward*
"Move **back**! Move out of the road! The bus is coming past!"

# backwards

Robert looked **backwards** over his shoulder at the dog.
The lion walked **backwards and forwards** in its cage.

# bad

**worse, worst**
**1** *not good*
The weather is very **bad** today. It is raining.
**2** **bad at**
Maria is good at maths, but she is **bad at** English.
**3** **bad for**
Eating a lot of sweets is **bad for** you.

# bag

Helen is putting some food into the **bag**.

# bake

**baking, baked, baked**
*to cook in an oven*
Anne **baked** some cakes this morning.

# baker

A **baker** makes bread.
Jane bought some bread at the **baker's**.

# bald

*without hair*
Helen's grandfather is **bald**.

# ball

Kate is playing with a **ball**.

# balloon

*a large bag with gas in it that goes up in the air*
The children saw a **balloon** in the sky yesterday.

# banana

*a long yellow fruit*
**Bananas** grow in hot places.

# bank

**1** *the side of a river*
Nick walked along the **bank** of the river.
**2** *a place where you can keep money*
At the end of the day, the shopkeeper took his money to the **bank**.

# bar

bar

bar of chocolate

**1** *a long piece of wood or metal*
There are **bars** in front of this window.
**2** Tom is eating a **bar** of chocolate.

# barber

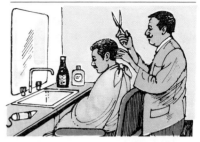

*a person who cuts men's hair*
The **barber** is cutting Robert's hair. Robert is at the **barber's**.

# baseball

*a game for two teams that you play with a ball*
Many Americans play **baseball**.

# basket

Alice is carrying fruit and vegetables in her **basket**.

# basketball

*a game for two teams that you play with a ball*
My brothers like playing **basketball**.

# bat

**1** *a small animal with wings*
**Bats** sleep in the day and fly at night.

**2** We use a **bat** when we hit a ball.

# bath

There is a **bath** in the bathroom.

# bathroom

*a room in a house*
We wash in the **bathroom**.

# battery

*plural* **batteries**
*a box that makes electricity*
I need a new **battery** for my radio.
Every car has a **battery**.

# be

is, being, was, been
**1** I **am** from Spain.
You **are** English.
He **is** a teacher.
She **is** a teacher, too.
It **is** very hot today.
We **are** hot.
You **are** students.
They **are** in our class.
Yesterday I **was** in London.
You **were** at home.
**2** Helen **is** sitting at her desk.
"What **are** you doing, Helen?"
– "I **am** writing a letter."

# beach

*plural* **beaches**

Some children are playing on the **beach**.

# bean

*a vegetable*
We had lamb, potatoes, and green **beans** for dinner.

# bear

*a large animal*
**Bears** have a lot of hair on their bodies.

# beard

Christopher has a **beard**.

beard

# beat

**beating, beat, beaten**
*to win against*
Our school played football against another school yesterday. Our team **beat** the other team, 3-1.

# beautiful

*very nice to look at*
I like your dress. It's very **beautiful**.

# became

*past of* **become**
David **became** a doctor in 1983.

# because

**1** "Why were you late for school today?" – "**Because** the bus was late."
**2 Because of** the rain, we didn't go outside.

# become

**becoming, became, become**
*to grow or change into*
"Look at this small plant," said the teacher. "It will **become** a tree in twenty years."

# bed

We sleep on a **bed**.

Alan **goes to bed** very late. He goes upstairs at eleven o'clock.

7

# bedroom

*a room in a house*
We sleep in the **bedroom**.
Our house has two **bedrooms**.

# bee

*a black and
yellow insect*
This is a **bee**.

# beef

*the meat of cows*
We had some **beef** and onions
for dinner.

# been

**1** *part of* **be**
Andrew bought his shop ten
years ago. He has **been** a
shopkeeper for ten years.
**2** *gone and come back again*
"Have you **been** to America?"
– "Yes. I went there in 1983."

# before

**1** Monday comes **before**
Tuesday. Wednesday comes
after Tuesday.
**2** "Have you been to England
**before**?" – "No, this is the first
time."

# began

*past of* **begin**
The film **began** at seven
o'clock.

# begin

**beginning, began, begun**
The start of the lesson is at nine
o'clock. The lesson **begins** at
nine o'clock. It ends at ten
o'clock.

# beginning

At the **beginning** of the day we
have breakfast.

# begun

*part of* **begin**
"Has the film **begun**?" – "No,
not yet."

# behind

The
blackboard is
**behind** the
teacher. The
teacher is in
front of the
blackboard.

# being

*part of* **be**
The new school is now **being**
built. It will be finished next
year.

# believe

**believing, believed, believed**
*to think that something is true*
"I've got a snake in my
pocket." – "No, you haven't! I
don't **believe** you."

# bell

At our school,
a **bell** rings
before each
lesson.

# belong to

This is my book. It **belongs to**
me.

# below

**1** *under*
The picture of
my father is
**below** the
picture of my
family.

**2** *at a lower place*
There are some names **below**:
    David
    Isabel
    Susan

# belt

*something you
wear round the
middle of your
body*
Tom has a leather **belt**.

# bend

**bending, bent, bent**
*to make something not straight*
We **bend** our legs when we sit
down.

# bent

*past and part of* **bend**
Martin **bent** the piece of wire.

# beside

*next to*
Jenny is sitting **beside** her
grandmother.

# best

**1** I like oranges and apples, but
I like bananas **best**.
**2** Peter, Michael, and Nick are
all good swimmers, but Peter is
a better swimmer than Michael
and Nick. Peter is the **best**
swimmer.

# better

**1** Alan is good at English, but
Tom is very good. Tom is
**better** at English than Alan.
**2** Peter is a **better** swimmer
than Michael.

# between

Lisa is standing **between** her father and mother.

# beyond

*on the other side of*
The village is **beyond** the hill. You can see it from the top of the hill.

# bicycle

Peter is on his **bicycle**.
**Bike** is another word for **bicycle**.

# big

**bigger, biggest**
*not small*
London is very **big**.
"How **big** is your school?" – "It's not very **big**. There are only a hundred students."

# bill

*a piece of paper that tells you how much you must pay*
My father pays the electricity **bill** every month.

The waiter brought the **bill** and Peter gave him the money.

# biology

In the **biology** lesson we learn about animals and plants.

# bird

**Birds** can fly.

# birth

**1 birth certificate**
A **birth certificate** tells you when a person was born.
**2 date of birth**
"What's your **date of birth**, please?" asked the doctor. "I was born on January the second, 1971."

# birthday

Today is Helen's **birthday**. She is sixteen years old. She was born on this day sixteen years ago.

# biscuit

*a small thin hard cake*
Alan likes eating **biscuits**.

# bit

*noun*
**1** *a small piece or amount*
Lisa had a **bit** of bread and cheese for lunch.
**2** "How old is your sister?" – "She's a **bit** older than me. I'm sixteen, and she's seventeen."
*verb*
**3** *past of* **bite**
The dog **bit** the man.

# bite

**biting, bit, bitten**
*to cut with the teeth*
A dog **bit** Helen when she was going to school.

# bitter

*not sweet*
There isn't any sugar in my coffee. The coffee is **bitter**.

# black

*the colour of the sky at night*
*noun*
**1 Black** is my favourite colour.
*adjective*
**2** The taxis in London are **black**.

# blackboard

The teacher is writing on the **blackboard**.

# blanket

Peter is putting some **blankets** on his bed.

# blew

*past of* **blow**
There was a lot of wind yesterday. The wind **blew** my hat off my head.

# blind

*not able to see*
My grandmother is **blind**. She cannot see.

# block

Robert lives in a **block** of flats.

# blood

I cut my arm and a lot of **blood** came out. My shirt was red with **blood**.

# blouse

Helen is wearing a new **blouse**.

blouse

# blow

**blowing, blew, blown**

**1** The wind **blew** all day yesterday. My hat **blew** off my head.
**2** The wind **blew** my hat off my head.

Nick **blew** the butterfly off his hand.

# blue

*the colour of the sky in the day*
*noun*
**1 Blue** is my favourite colour.
*adjective* **bluer, bluest**
**2** Robert's car is **blue**.

# board

board

We are playing a game on the **board**.

# boat

The men are in the **boat**. They are catching fish.

# body

*plural* **bodies**
**1** Dogs have hair all over their **bodies**.
**2** *a dead person*
The police found a **body** in the old house.

# boil

**1** "Robert, the water is **boiling**. You can make the tea now."
**2** "What are you cooking?" – "I'm **boiling** some potatoes for our dinner."

# bone

The dog is eating a **bone**.

bone

# book

Maria is reading a **book**.

# bookcase

*a place where we put books*
There are a lot of books in this **bookcase**.

# bookshop

We buy books in a **bookshop**.

# boot

This is a pair of **boots**.

# bored

*not interested*
"What did you do in the school holidays, Susan?" – "I did nothing, and I didn't see any friends. I was very **bored**."

# boring

*not interesting*
I didn't like that film. It was very **boring**.

# born

Peter was **born** on November the tenth, 1971. His birthday is on November the tenth.

# borrow

Nick didn't have a pen. He **borrowed** a pen from Tom. He gave it back to Tom after the lesson.

# both

Kate has got two brothers. They are **both** students at London University. **Both of** them study medicine.

# bottle

There is some water in the **bottle**.

# bottom

*noun*
**1** Alan is at the **bottom** of the stairs. Helen is at the top of the stairs.

*adjective*
**2** *the lowest*
"Where are the books?" – "In the **bottom** cupboard."

# bought

*past and part of* **buy**
Anne **bought** some fruit at the market yesterday.

# bowl

There are some eggs in the **bowl**.

# box

*plural* **boxes**

David bought a new television. He took the television out of the **box**.

# boy

Peter and Paul are **boys**. Lisa is a girl.

# bracket

These are **brackets** ( )
We sometimes use **brackets** when we write:
Seven plus eight equals fifteen (7 + 8 = 15).

# brain

*the part of the head we use for thinking*

# branch

*plural* **branches**

This bird is sitting on a **branch**.

# brave

**braver, bravest**
Kate saw a snake. She did not run away. She was very **brave**.

# bread

We eat a lot of **bread**. We buy **bread** from the baker.

# break

*verb* **breaking, broke, broken**
**1** Robert dropped the cup and it **broke**.
**2** The ball **broke** the window.

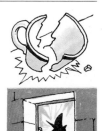

**3 to break down**
Steven's car **broke down** when he was coming home. The car stopped and would not move. Steven walked home.
*noun*
**4** In the mornings at school we have a **break** between lessons. The **break** is ten minutes long.

# breakfast

We have **breakfast** in the morning. We have lunch in the middle of the day. We have dinner in the evening.

# breath

*air that you take into your body*
"Take a deep **breath** before you go under the water."

# breathe

**breathing, breathed, breathed**
*to take air into your body*
We cannot live without air. We must **breathe**.

# brick

The men built a house with **bricks**.
Our house is made of **brick**.

# bride

*a woman who is going to be married today*
Isabel is getting married this afternoon. She is the **bride**.

# bridge

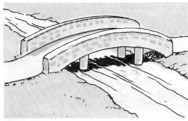

There is a **bridge** across the river.

# briefcase

Christopher carries paper and pens in his **briefcase**.

# bright

**1** *giving a lot of light*
The sun is very **bright**. The light in my room is not very **bright**.
**2** *not dark*
Yellow, red, and orange are **bright** colours. Brown and black are dark colours.

# bring

**bringing, brought, brought**

"Helen, **bring** me your book!" said the teacher.
The postman **brings** letters to our house every day.

# broad

From one side of the river to the other is twenty metres. The river is twenty metres **broad**.

# broke

*past of* **break**
The ball **broke** the window.

# broken

*verb*
**1** *part of* **break**
Robert has **broken** the window.
*adjective*
**2** Michael fell off the wall. Now he has got a **broken** leg.

# brother

Peter and Lisa have the same mother and father. Peter is Lisa's **brother**. Lisa is Peter's sister.

# brought

*past and part of* **bring**
"How did you come to school today?" – "My father **brought** me in his car."

# brown

*the colour of coffee*
*noun*
**1 Brown** is my favourite colour.
*adjective*
**2** Maria has **brown** eyes.

# brush

*plural* **brushes**

brush

Martin is painting the wall. He is using a **brush**.

# bucket

We can carry water in a **bucket**.

# buffalo

*plural* **buffaloes**

*a large animal*
This is a **buffalo**. It is a **water buffalo**.

# build

**building, built, built**

These men are **building** a house.

# builder

*a person who builds*
"What's your job?" – "I'm a **builder**. I build houses."

# building

You can see six **buildings** in this street.

# built

*past and part of* **build**
The men **built** a bridge across the river.

# bunch

*plural* **bunches**
*a lot of things together*
This is a **bunch** of grapes.
Lisa bought a **bunch** of bananas in the market.

# burn

**burning, burnt** *or* **burned, burnt** *or* **burned**

**1** The piece of paper is **burning**.

**2** The men **burnt** some old chairs on the fire.

# burst

**bursting, burst, burst**

*to come open suddenly*
"There are too many things in that bag. It will **burst**!"

# bus

*plural* **buses**

*plural* **buses**
**1** There are some students on the **bus**. They are going to school.
**2 bus station**
We went to the **bus station** to get the bus to Scotland.
**3 bus stop**
We get on and off the bus at the **bus stop**.

# bush

*plural* **bushes**

There is a **bush** near the road.

# busier

Yesterday I was very busy, but today I am even **busier**.

# business

*plural* **businesses**
Sam has a small **business**. He makes shoes, and he sells them in the market.

# busy

**busier, busiest**
Christopher is doing a lot of work. He is very **busy** today.

# but

I waited for the bus, **but** it didn't come.

# butcher

A **butcher** sells meat.
Susan bought some meat at the **butcher's**.

# butter

*something that we make from milk*
**Butter** is yellow. We put **butter** on bread.

# butterfly

*plural* **butterflies**

*an insect*
This **butterfly** has red and yellow wings.

# button

There are five **buttons** on the front of this shirt.

button

# buy

**buying, bought, bought**

Alice is **buying** some fruit.
My uncle has **bought** me a bicycle.

# by

**1** Helen goes to school **by** bus.
**2** "Hamlet" is **by** William Shakespeare.
**3** *next to*
The lamp is on the table **by** the bed.
**4** *before*
It gets dark here after half past six. **By** seven o'clock, it is night.
**5 by myself**
*without any other person*
I walk to school **by myself** every day.
I did the work **by myself**. No one helped me.

# C c

## cabbage

*a green vegetable*
**Cabbages** have big leaves.

## cafe

Nick and Tom are in a **cafe**.
They are having an ice cream.

## cage

*a place where we keep birds or animals*
The lions in the zoo live in **cages**.

## cake

*a sweet food*
Peter likes eating **cake**.

## calendar

| JUNE | | 1987 | | | |
|---|---|---|---|---|---|
| S | 2 | 9 | 16 | 23 | 30 |
| M | 3 | 10 | 17 | 24 | |
| T | 4 | 11 | 18 | 25 | |
| W | 5 | 12 | 19 | 26 | |
| T | 6 | 13 | 20 | 27 | |
| F | 7 | 14 | 21 | 28 | |
| S | 1 | 8 | 15 | 22 | 29 |

*a piece of paper that shows us the days, weeks, and months of the year*
"Is June 10th a Monday?" – "I don't know. Look at the **calendar**."

## calf

*plural* **calves**
*a young cow*
Martin's cow has a **calf**.

## call

1 Jane **called** her children.
"Come here!" she said.
2 *to give a name to*
Louise and James **called** their new baby Lucy.

## calves

*plural of* **calf**
There were some **calves** in the field.

## came

*past of* **come**
My family **came** to this town ten years ago.

## camel

*a large animal*
**Camels** can live in the desert.

## camera

Helen took some photos with her **camera**.

## camp

*verb*
1 *to live in a tent for a holiday*
Tom and Nick are **camping** in a tent near the sea.
*noun*
2 **holiday camp**
Jenny is at a **holiday camp**. There are lots of children to play with and many nice things to do every day.

## can

*verb* **could**
1 Cars **can** move faster than bicycles.
My young brother **can** write Spanish, but he can't write English.
2 "**Can** I go to the cinema tomorrow?" – "Yes, you **can** go if you do all your work first."
*noun*
3 Lisa bought a **can** of tomatoes in the market.

## cannot or can't

1 Babies **cannot** read or write.
2 Tom **cannot** play football today because he is ill.

## cap

John is wearing a **cap** on his head.

## capital

*noun*
1 *the most important town in a country*
London is the **capital** of England.
Madrid is the **capital** of Spain.
*adjective*
2 A, E, T are **capital** letters.
a, e, t are small letters.

## captain

*a man who controls a ship or a plane*
My uncle is the **captain** of a ship.

# car

**1** Robert is driving his **car**.
**2 car park**
*a place where you can leave a car for a short time*
Christopher left his car in the **car park** of the hotel.

# card

*a piece of thick paper*
The teacher's name is on a **card** outside his door.

# care

**caring, cared, cared**
*to think that something is important*
"It's raining, but I don't **care**. I'm going out to play football."

# careful

Robert is a very **careful** driver.
"There are eggs in this bag. Be **careful** when you carry it!"

# carefully

Robert drives his car very **carefully**. He does not go too fast.

# carpenter

Martin is a **carpenter**. He is making a door.

# carpet

Steven has got a new **carpet**. He is going to put the **carpet** on the floor of his living room.

# carried

*past and part of* **carry**
Michael **carried** the bags for his mother.

# carrot

*a long orange vegetable*
We buy **carrots** in the greengrocer's.

# carry

**carries, carrying, carried, carried**

**1** Tom is **carrying** some books.

**2 to carry on**
*to continue*
The lesson ended, but Kate **carried on** reading her book. She read her book until the start of the next lesson.

# cart

The donkey is pulling a **cart**.

# cartoon

**1** *a drawing that makes you laugh*
Tom is laughing at a **cartoon** of a dog that is trying to catch a cat.
**2** *a film that is made by putting many drawings together*
Jenny is watching a Walt Disney **cartoon** on television.

# case

*a large bag that you put clothes in*
When Lisa went on holiday, she took two **cases**.

**Case** is a short way of saying **suitcase**.

# cassette

**1** Helen is holding a **cassette**.
**2 cassette recorder**
Helen is putting a cassette in the **cassette recorder**.

# castle

*a big strong building that was used in times of war*
There is a famous **castle** at Edinburgh in Scotland.

# cat

*a small animal*
This is a **cat**.

# catch

**catches, catching, caught, caught**

**1** *to take a moving thing in your hand*
Kate is **catching** the ball.

Simon's dog ran across the road. He ran after it and **caught** it.
**2** Alan **catches** the bus to school at eight o'clock.
**3** Michael went fishing today. He **caught** a fish.
**4** Helen **caught** a cold. She was ill for two days.
**5 to catch up with**
*to run after someone and join him*
Nick ran fast, but he couldn't **catch up with** the other boys.

# caught

*past and part of* **catch**
"Which train did you catch?" – "I **caught** the five o'clock train."

# cave

There is a **cave** in the hill here.

cave

# ceiling

Martin is painting the **ceiling**.

# cement

The men built a house with bricks. They put **cement** between the bricks.

# centigrade

*a measurement of temperature*
It is very hot today. It is thirty degrees **centigrade** (30°C).

# centimetre

*a measurement of length*
One hundred **centimetres** equal one metre (100 **cm** = 1m).
Helen's pencil is twelve **centimetres** long.

# centre

*the middle*
The cinema is in the **centre** of the town.

# century

*plural* **centuries**
*a hundred years*
The Colosseum in Rome was built many **centuries** ago.
Shakespeare lived in the sixteenth **century**.

# certain

*sure*
"Where's Martin? I am **certain** that he told me to meet him here at two o'clock, but he's not here."

# certainly

*of course*
"Could you go to the shops, please, Tom?" – "Yes, **certainly!**"

# chain

*a line of metal rings joined together*
A bicycle has a **chain**. The **chain** makes the wheels turn.

# chair

Lisa is sitting on a **chair**.

# chalk

The teacher writes on the blackboard with **chalk**.

# chance

There is a **chance** that my uncle will return from London today. Perhaps he will return. We do not know.

# change

*verb* **changing, changed, changed**
**1** *to become different*
This town has **changed** a lot in the last ten years.

**2** Before he plays football, Nick **changes** his clothes.
**3** "Does this train go to Bristol?" – "No, you must **change** at London."
*noun*
**4** *things that are different*
When Martin came back to the village after many years, he saw a lot of **changes**.

# channel

In England there are four television **channels**. There are four different programmes at the same time.

# chapter

*a part of a book*
This book has fifteen **chapters**. I am reading **chapter** four.

# character

*a person in a book or a film*
Sindbad is a famous **character** in some stories.

# chart

*a piece of paper which has numbers or information on it*
There is a **chart** on the wall of our classroom. It shows how many students there are in each class.

# chase

**chasing, chased, chased**

This little girl is **chasing** her dog.

# cheap

*not costing a lot of money*
A bicycle is **cheap**. A car is not **cheap**. It is expensive.

# cheat

The man in the market **cheated** me. I paid him eight pounds for the shirt, but the price was really five pounds.

# check

*to make sure that something is all right*
The students did the exercise. Then the teacher **checked** their answers.
Steven **checks** his car before he drives to London.

# cheek

*a part of the face*
Robert ran very fast. Now his **cheeks** are red.

# cheer

**1** *to shout because you are pleased*
The crowd **cheered** when they saw the football team.
**2** "**Cheer up!**"
Michael lost his bicycle. "Don't be sad," his friend said to him. "**Cheer up!** We'll find it!"

# cheese

We buy **cheese** at the grocer's. **Cheese** comes from milk.

# chemist

My father is a **chemist**. He makes medicines and sells them to people who are ill.
Kate was feeling ill. She went to the **chemist's** and bought some medicine.

# chemistry

In **chemistry** lessons we learn about gases, metals, and liquids.

# chess

*a game that you play on a board*
Nick likes playing **chess**.

# chest

**1** *the front part of the body*
The ball hit Tom in the **chest**.
**2** *a large box*
Helen puts her clothes in a **chest**.

# chicken

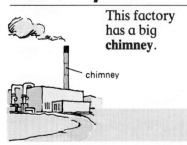

*a bird*
We get eggs from **chickens**. We can eat **chickens**, too.

# child

*plural* **children**
Louise has a new baby. It is her first **child**.

# children

*plural of* **child**
"How old are your **children**, Jane?" – "Peter is fourteen, Lisa is thirteen, and Paul is ten."

# chimney

This factory has a big **chimney**.

chimney

# chin

chin

*a part of the face*
This is Kate's **chin**.

# chocolate

*a sweet food or drink*
Peter likes eating **chocolate**.

# choose

**choosing, chose, chosen**
"You can have fruit, cheese, or ice cream. **Choose** one." –
"Cheese, please."

# Christmas

**1** *December 25th*
In many countries, **Christmas Day** is a holiday. People give presents and eat nice food.
**2** *a holiday on the days around December 25th*
I am going to see my aunt for a week at **Christmas**.

# cinema

Nick is going to the **cinema** tonight. He is going to see a new film.

# circle

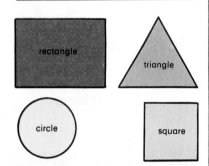

rectangle

triangle

circle

square

A **circle** is round.

# circus

*plural* **circuses**

You can see a lot of animals and dancers at a **circus**.

# city

*plural* **cities**
*a large town*
Madrid and London are **cities**.

# clap

**clapping, clapped, clapped**

The children liked the puppets. Now they are **clapping**.

# class

*plural* **classes**
There are fifteen boys and ten girls in my **class** at school.
We must not talk **in class**.

# classroom

You can see a blackboard, a table, and some desks in the **classroom**.

# clean

*adjective*
**1** After he played football, Peter washed his dirty shirt. Now his shirt is **clean** and he can wear it again.

*verb*
**2** Jane is **cleaning** the windows.

Nick **cleans** his teeth every morning and every evening.

# clear

**1** *easy to understand*
This is a very **clear** book. I can understand everything in it.
**2** *not cloudy*
On a **clear** night, you can see all the stars in the sky.

# clerk

"What's your job?" – "I'm a **clerk**. I work in an office."

# clever

Susan is very **clever**. She knows a lot of things. She can answer all the teacher's questions.

# climate

*the weather that a place has*
Egypt has a hot dry **climate**.

# climb

*verb*
**1** The men **climbed** the high mountain.
Nick likes **climbing** trees.
*noun*
**2** Tom and Peter walked up the steep hill. After the **climb**, they were very hot.

# clock

"What's the time?" – "Look at the **clock**! It is half past two."

# close 1

*near*
Alan lives **close** to the school. He can walk there in five minutes.

# close 2

**closing, closed, closed**
*to shut*
"The windows are open. Please **close** the windows when you leave."

# closed

*not open*
We don't go to school on Sundays. The school is **closed**.

# cloth

Jenny is cutting some **cloth**. She is making a dress.

cloth

# clothes

"Did you buy some new **clothes**?" – "Yes. I bought two shirts and some trousers."

# cloud

There are some **clouds** in the sky.

# cloudy

**cloudier, cloudiest**
It is **cloudy** today. There are a lot of clouds in the sky.

# club

There is a sports **club** in our town. People go there to play tennis and other games.

# coal

We get **coal** from under the ground. It is hard and black. We can make fires with it.

# coast

*land next to the sea*
Venice is a city on the **coast** of Italy.

# coat

coat

Christopher is wearing a **coat**.

# coconut

**Coconuts** grow on palm trees.

# code

*a secret way of writing*
Peter used numbers for his **code**: A = 1, B = 2, C = 3, etc. He wrote his name **in code**: 16 5 20 5 18.

# coffee

Mark is drinking a cup of **coffee**.

# coin

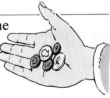

Nick has some **coins** in his hand.

# cold

*adjective*
**1** It is **cold** outside today. Michael is **cold**.

*noun*
**2** Kate feels ill. She has got a **cold**.

# collar

This is a shirt **collar**.

This is a dog **collar**.

# collect

*to bring together*
After the lesson, Alan **collected** the books and gave them to the teacher.

# collection

Peter has a large **collection** of old coins. He has got 300 coins.

# college

*a place where people study after they have left school*
My brother wants to be an engineer. He is studying at a **college**.

# colour

"What **colour** is your new car?" – "It's red."

# coloured

Peter has a box of **coloured** pencils. Each pencil is a different colour.

# comb

*verb*
**1** Nick is **combing** his hair.
*noun*
**2** Nick is using a **comb**.

# come

**coming, came, come**
**1** Alan **comes** to our house by bus.
My sister goes to school at nine o'clock. She **comes home** at three o'clock.

"Helen, **come here**! Bring me your book!"
**2** "D" **comes** before "E" in the alphabet.
Tuesday **comes** after Monday.

**3 to come back**
Michael left here on Monday. He went to London. He **came back** on Friday.
**4 to come from**
Nick is French. He **comes from** Paris.
**5 "Come on!"**
*"Hurry!"*
"**Come on**, Nick! We're late for the bus!"

# comfortable

I like this soft chair. It's very **comfortable**.

# comic

Jenny is reading a **comic**.

# comma

These are **commas** ,,,,
There is a **comma** in this sentence:
Helen likes bananas, but she does not like oranges.

# common

Camels are very **common** in Egypt. You can see them in many places.

# company

*plural* **companies**
My father works for a big **company**. The **company** makes farm machines.

# comparative

Most adjectives have a **comparative** and a superlative. The **comparative** of "hot" is "hotter". The superlative of "hot" is "hottest".
Today it is *hotter* than it was yesterday.

# compare

**comparing, compared, compared**
*to see if two or more things are the same or different*
Alan **compared** the two cars: "The red car is bigger than the blue car."

# competition

There was a **competition** to find the best student of Spanish in the school. Susan got all the answers right. She won the **competition**.

# complain

*to say that you are angry because you do not like something*
The food was very bad. Robert **complained** to the waiter.

# composition

*a short piece of writing*
The student wrote a **composition** about his holiday. Then he gave it to the teacher.

# concert

*music played for people who come to listen to it*
These people are at a **concert**.

# concrete

*sand, stones, cement, and water put together*
The men built some new offices using **concrete**.

## consist of

The United Kingdom **consists of** four countries: England, Wales, Scotland, and Northern Ireland.

## consonant

These English letters are called **consonants: b, c, d, f, g, h, j, k, l, m, n, p, q, r, s, t, v, w, x, y, z.** The letters a, e, i, o, and u are called vowels.

## contain

*to have inside*
That bottle **contains** one litre of water.

## continent

Africa and Europe are **continents**. There are many countries in Africa and in Europe.

## continue

**continuing, continued, continued**
*to do something for more time*
Susan stopped working when her uncle came in. "Don't stop working, Susan. Please **continue**," he said.

## control

**controlling, controlled, controlled**
There was a lot of water on the road. The driver could not **control** his car, and it hit a wall.

## conversation

Peter and Tom are having a **conversation**. They are talking about football.

## cook

Louise is **cooking** some meat and vegetables.

## cooker

Louise is cooking some meat and vegetables on the **cooker**.

## cooking

"Who does the **cooking** in your house?" – "My mother cooks most days, and I sometimes do the **cooking** too."

## cool

*not warm, but not cold*
In the morning and evening, the air is **cool**.

## copy

*verb* **copies, copying, copied, copied**

1 Helen is **copying** the words from the blackboard.
*noun, plural* **copies**
2 The clerk made three **copies** of the important letter.

## corn

Farmers grow **corn** in fields. We make flour from **corn**.

## corner

Mark is waiting at the **corner** of the street.

## correct

*adjective*
**1** *right*
Susan did the work very well. All her answers are **correct**.
*verb*
**2** *to make right*
Lisa did some work, and gave it to the teacher. The teacher **corrected** the answers that were wrong.

## cost

*verb* **costing, cost, cost**
1 "How much does this pen **cost**?" – "It **costs** fifty pence."
*noun*
2 The **cost** of this pen is fifty pence.

## cotton

*noun*
1 *a cloth that clothes are made from*
Kate's dress is made of **cotton**.
*adjective*
2 Tom likes wearing **cotton** shirts.

# cough

*noun*
1 Lisa has a **cough**. Her mother is giving her some medicine.
*verb*
2 Lisa is **coughing**. She has got a cold.

# could

1 *past of* **can**
Peter **could** swim when he was five.
2 "**Could** you close the door, please?" – "Yes, of course."
"**Could** I have some more tea, please?" – "I'm sorry, but there isn't any."
3 If I had enough money, I **could** visit my brother in America.

# couldn't

*could not*
Susan **couldn't** go to school yesterday, because she was ill.

# count

Lisa **counted** the eggs: "One … two … three … four … five … six. There are six eggs."

# country

1 *plural* **countries**
"Which **country** do you come from?" – "I come from Spain."
2 **the country**
Michael doesn't live in a town. He lives in **the country**. He works on a farm.

# course

1 *a part of a meal*
We sometimes have three **courses** for dinner: a fish **course**, a meat **course**, and a sweet **course**.
2 The plane was flying to London, but then it changed **course** and flew to Paris.
3 **of course**
"Did you go to school today?" – "Yes, **of course** I did."

# cousin

*a child of your aunt and uncle*
Peter and Lisa are my **cousins**. They are the children of my Uncle Steven and Aunt Jane.

# cover

Nick is **covering** the food to keep it hot.

# cow

There are three **cows** in the field.

# crack

*noun*
1 There is a **crack** in this plate.
*verb*
2 Peter **cracked** this plate when he dropped it.

# crash

**crashes, crashing, crashed, crashed**

Robert's lorry **crashed** into a wall. Now he cannot drive it.

# cream

*the part of the milk that goes to the top*
Lisa likes to eat fruit and **cream**.

# cried

*past and part of* **cry**
The little girl **cried** when she fell down and cut her leg.

# criminal

*a person who does something that is against the law*
The police caught the **criminal**.

# crop

*food that a farmer grows*
The corn **crop** was bad this year. The farmers did not get much corn from their fields.

# cross

*verb* **crosses, crossing, crossed, crossed**
1 *to go from one side of something to the other side*
Peter **crosses** the road carefully.
*noun, plural* **crosses**
2 This is a **cross** ×.
The students do exercises in their books. If an answer is wrong, the teacher puts a **cross** after it.

# crowd

*a lot of people*
There was a big **crowd** at the football game.

# cruel

**crueller, cruellest**
That man is very **cruel**. He laughed when the boy fell off his bicycle and broke his leg.

## cry

**cries, crying, cried, cried**
The little girl fell down in the street. Now she is **crying**.

## cup

Nick is drinking from a **cup**. He is drinking a **cup** of tea.

## cupboard

Peter is looking in the **cupboard**.

## curtain

*a piece of cloth that you pull in front of a window at night*

There are **curtains** at the window of Helen's house.

## curved

*not straight*
The road to our village is **curved**.

## Customs

*where people look at the things that you bring into a country*
David is at the airport. He is going through **Customs**.

## cut

*verb* **cutting, cut, cut**

**1** David is **cutting** the bread with a knife.

**2** Nick fell down and **cut** his arm. He had blood on his shirt.
**3 to cut down**
The men **cut down** the tree near our house yesterday and burnt it.
**4 to cut up**
*to cut into small pieces*
Maria **cut up** the vegetables before cooking them.
**5 to cut out**
"I like the picture in your book. Can I **cut** it **out** and put it on the wall?"
*noun*
**6** Alan fell off his bicycle. Now he has a **cut** on his leg.

# D d

## dad or daddy

*a name that children call their father*
"Can I have an apple, **daddy**?" said the little girl. "Of course," said her father.

## dance

*verb* **dancing, danced, danced**

**1** The children are **dancing**.
*noun*
**2** The children are doing a **dance**.

## dancer

*a person who dances*
We saw some **dancers** at the theatre yesterday.

## danger

This sign tells us that there is **danger**. We must not go near the railway.

# dangerous

Children must not play near the railway. It is very **dangerous**.

# dark

*adjective*
**1** *not light*
At night the sky is **dark**.

"What colour is Peter's bicycle?" – "It's **dark** blue."
**2** *not fair*
Kate's hair is **dark**. It is nearly black.
*noun*
**3** You cannot see very well in the **dark**. There is no light.

# date

**1** *a brown fruit*
**Dates** grow on palm trees.
**2** "What's the **date** today?" – "It's the ninth of May."
**3 date of birth**
Helen was born on July the third, nineteen seventy-one (July 3rd, 1971). This is her **date of birth**.

# daughter

This is Lisa with her mother and father. She is their **daughter**.

# day

**1** There are seven **days** in a week: Sunday, Monday, Tuesday, Wednesday, Thursday, Friday, and Saturday.
I get up at seven o'clock every **day**.
**2** In the **day**, the sun shines in the sky. At night, you can see the moon.

# dead

David did not give his plants any water. Now the plants are **dead**.
The dog is **dead** because a car hit it.

# deaf

*not able to hear*
The old man is nearly **deaf**. He can hear loud noises, but he cannot hear people when they talk to him.

# dear

**1** Sam wrote a letter to Robert. He started: "**Dear** Robert, …"
**2** A **dear** friend is a very good friend.
**3** This shirt was very **dear**. It cost twenty pounds.
**4** "**Oh dear!**"
We say "**Oh dear!**" when something bad happens: "I broke my glasses today." – "**Oh dear!**"

# December

*the twelfth month of the year*
There are thirty-one days in **December**.

# decide

**deciding, decided, decided**
"Do you want to buy the brown shoes or the black shoes?" – "I don't know. I can't **decide**."

# deep

*going down a long way*
The sea is very **deep**. Rivers are not very **deep**.

# degree

*a measurement of heat or temperature*
It is hot today. The temperature is thirty-five **degrees**. You can write thirty-five **degrees** like this: 35°.

# deliver

*to take something to a house, factory, or office*
The postman **delivered** four letters to our house today.

# dentist

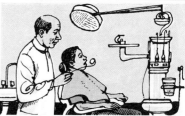

*a person who looks after your teeth*
My tooth hurt. I went to the **dentist**.

# depth

"What is the **depth** of the river here?" – "The river is seven metres deep."

# describe

**describing, described, described**
*to say what someone or something looks like*

"Tom, can you **describe** your sister?" – "Yes. She is small and thin, and has dark hair."

# description

*what someone or something looks like*
The policeman asked me for a **description** of the man who took my wallet.

# desert

In the **desert** there is a lot of sand. There are not many plants or trees because there is no water.

# desk

Susan is sitting at her **desk**. She is doing some work in her book.

# diagram

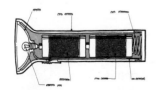

*a picture that shows you how a thing works*
This is a **diagram** of a torch.

# dial

*noun*
**1** *the round part of a telephone with numbers on it*
*verb* **dialling, dialled, dialled**
**2** Steven is **dialling** the number of his office.

# dialogue

*two people talking to each other*
We sometimes listen to a **dialogue** in our French lesson.

# diamond

*a white or yellow stone that costs a lot of money*

Isabel wears a **diamond** ring. There is a big **diamond** in her ring.

# diary

*plural* **diaries**
*a book which you write in at the end of each day*
Kate went to the zoo today. She wrote about it in her **diary**.

# dictionary

*plural* **dictionaries**
*a book that tells you the meaning of words*
"What does 'jewel' mean?" – "I don't know. Look in the **dictionary**."

# did

*past of* **do**
"**Did** you go to the cinema last night?" – "Yes, we **did**."
I **did** my homework before dinner.

# didn't

*did not*
Robert **didn't** go to work yesterday, because he was ill.

# die

**dying, died, died**
Tom's grandmother is dead. She **died** in 1984. She was eighty-six years old.

# difference

"What's the **difference** between a horse and a donkey?" – "A horse is bigger than a donkey, and a horse has shorter ears than a donkey."

# different

These keys are **different**.

These keys are not **different**. They are the same.

# differently

People and animals walk **differently**. People walk on two legs, animals walk on four legs.

# difficult

"Mother, why is the sky blue?" – "That's a **difficult** question, Paul. I can't answer it."

# dig

**digging, dug, dug**
Mark is **digging** in his garden.

# dining room

*a room in a house*
"Come into the **dining room**. We're going to have lunch."

# dinner

We have breakfast in the morning. We have **dinner** in the evening.

# dirty

**dirtier, dirtiest**
Peter played football this morning. He fell down. Now he is very **dirty**. He must have a wash.

# disappear

*not to be seen*
"Where did you go?" said Susan. "You were with me in the shop, but then you **disappeared**!"

# disappointed

When you want something, but you do not get it, you are **disappointed**.
Lisa was **disappointed** because her father didn't bring her a present from America.

# discover

**1** *to find something for the first time*
They **discovered** oil in America about sixty years ago.

**2** *to find out something*
We didn't know that Tom was ill. We **discovered** that he was in hospital when we spoke to his mother.

# disease

*an illness*
Young children get a lot of **diseases**.

# dish

*plural* **dishes**

dish

Michael is taking some food from the **dish**. He is putting it on his plate.

# dislike

**disliking, disliked, disliked**
*not to like*
Peter **dislikes** Alan. They are not friends.

# distance

The **distance** between London and Paris is 350 kilometres.

# dive

**diving, dived, dived**
*to go into water with your head first*
Peter can swim very well. He doesn't jump into the river. He **dives** in.

# divide

**dividing, divided, divided**
*to make into parts*
**1** We **divided** the orange between us.
**2** Twelve **divided by** three equals four ($12 \div 3 = 4$).

# do

**does, doing, did, done**
**1** "What's Helen **doing** now?" – "She's reading."
We have **done** our homework. Now we can watch television.
**2** I like oranges, but I **don't** like bananas.
**3** "**Don't** play games in the classroom!" said the teacher.
**4** "What **do** you have for breakfast?" – "I always have an egg and some tea."
"**Do** you go to school every day?" – "Yes, I **do**."
**5** "What **does** your father **do**, Alan?" – "He is a greengrocer."

# doctor

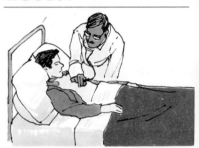

Tom is ill. The **doctor** is looking at him.

# does

*part of* **do**
"**Does** your sister like ice cream?" – "Yes, she **does**."
Tom **does** his homework before dinner.

# doesn't

*does not*
Martin **doesn't** like eggs.

# dog

*an animal*
The **dog** is sitting down.

# doing

*part of* **do**
"What are those men **doing**?"
– "They're building a wall."

# doll

This little girl is playing with her toys. She is giving her **doll** a drink.

# domestic science

*a school subject*
At school, Maria has lessons in **domestic science**. She learns about cooking and making clothes.

# done

*part of* **do**
"Have you **done** your work?" asked the teacher. "Yes, I have," said Peter.

# donkey

*an animal*
This **donkey** is pulling a cart.

# don't

*do not*
**1** I like oranges, but I **don't** like bananas.

**2** "**Don't** play in the road!"

# door

Helen is closing the **door**.

# down

*not up*
Alan is walking **down** the stairs. Helen is walking up the stairs.

# downstairs

Our house has two floors. We eat **downstairs**, and we sleep upstairs.
"Come **downstairs** and have your dinner!" Jane said to her children.

# downwards

*towards a lower place*
From here, the road goes down the hill. The road goes **downwards**.

# dozen

*twelve*
"A **dozen** eggs, please."

# Dr

*doctor*
We write **Dr** before the name of a doctor:
**Dr** Smith works in a hospital.

# drank

*past of* **drink**
I **drank** seven cups of tea yesterday.

# draw

*verb* **drawing, drew, drawn**

**1** Paul is **drawing** his house.

**2** The football teams got five goals each. The teams **drew**, 5-5.
*noun*
**3** The football match was a **draw**, 5-5.

# drawer

Helen is putting some clothes in the **drawer**.

# drawing

This is Paul's **drawing** of his house.

# drawn

*past of* **draw**
"Look, mother! I've **drawn** our house," said Paul.

# dream

*verb* **dreaming, dreamed** *or*
**dreamt, dreamed** *or* **dreamt**
**1** *to think about something
when you are sleeping*
Michael **dreamed** about
football last night.
*noun*
**2** Susan had a nice **dream**
about her holiday.

# dress

*plural* **dresses**
Kate is
wearing a
**dress**.

# dressed

**1** *wearing clothes*
Nick is **dressed** in his football
clothes.
**2 to get dressed**
*to put your clothes on*
In the morning, Martin
washes. Then he **gets dressed**
and has breakfast.

# drew

*past of* **draw**
Paul **drew** a picture of his
house at school yesterday.

# dried

*past and part of* **dry**
Tom's clothes were wet, but
the sun **dried** them quickly.

# drier

This shirt is **drier** than that
shirt. It will be dry in a minute.

# drink

*verb* **drinking,
drank, drunk**
**1** Susan is
**drinking** some
water.

*noun*
**2** "It's very hot. I need a **drink**.
Can I have a **drink** of water,
please?"

# drive

**driving, drove, driven**

David is **driving** his car. He is
taking Nick to school.

# driver

Robert does not drive too fast.
He is a good **driver**.
Frank is a lorry **driver**. His
work is driving a lorry.

# driving licence

*a piece of paper that says that
you can drive a car*
If you want to drive a car, you
must have a **driving licence**.

# drop

**dropping, dropped, dropped**

Alice has
**dropped** her
basket.

# drove

*past of* **drive**
Robert **drove** to London
yesterday.

# drum

This man is
playing his
**drums**.

# drunk

*part of* **drink**
"Have you **drunk** your tea?" –
"Yes, I have. Can I have some
more, please?"

# dry

*adjective* **drier, driest**
**1** The desert is very **dry**. There
is no water there.

*verb* **dries,
drying, dried,
dried**
**2** Peter is
**drying** his
hair.

# duck

*a bird*
There are two
**ducks** in the
picture.

# dug

*part and part of* **dig**
Last week Mark **dug** his
garden. Now he can put plants
in it.

# during

Frank works at night and
sleeps **during** the day.
Last night was very windy.
**During** the night a big tree fell
down.

## dust

Alice is sweeping **dust** off the floor.

## duster

Lisa is cleaning the blackboard with a **duster**.

## dying

*part of* **die**
Andrew's dog is very old. It is not strong. It is **dying**.

# E e

## each

**1** *every*
**Each** student has an exercise book for his work.
**2** *for one*
"How much do these pens cost?" – "They cost fifty pence **each**."
**3 each other**
Maria and Helen are friends. They like **each other**.

## eagle

*a large bird*
**Eagles** kill small animals.

## ear

ear

*a part of the face*
We hear things with our **ears**.

## early

**earlier, earliest**
**1** *before the right time*
School starts at nine o'clock, but Helen was there at half past eight. She was **early**.
**2** *near the start of the day*
Michael gets up **early** every morning.

## earn

*to get money by working*
Robert works in the evenings, and at weekends too. He **earns** a lot of money.

## earring

This lady is wearing **earrings**.

## earth

**1** Alice is putting some plants in the **earth** in her garden.

**2 The Earth** goes round the sun every year.

## easier

It is **easier** to read English than to write English.

## east

*noun*
**1** In the morning, the sun comes up in the **east**.
*adjective*
**2** Kenya is in **East** Africa.

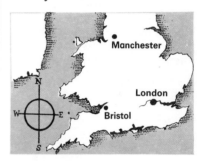

Manchester

London

W ← → E

Bristol

London is **east of** Bristol.

## eastern

London is in **eastern** England. The River Thames is in the **eastern** part of England.

## easy

**easier, easiest**
*not difficult*
These questions are very **easy**. All the students can answer them.

## eat

**eating, ate, eaten**

Alan is **eating** a banana.

# edge

1 The cat is near the **edge** of the roof.

2 I cut my finger on the **edge** of the knife.

# education

*teaching and learning*
David had a good **education**. He went to a good school and then to London University.

# egg

Nick likes eating **eggs**.

# eight

*the number* 8
There are **eight** bottles on the table.
Five plus three equals **eight** (5 + 3 = 8).

# eighteen

*the number* 18
My brother is **eighteen** years old.
Sixteen plus two equals **eighteen** (16 + 2 = 18).

# eighth

August is the **eighth** month of the year.
Alan's birthday is on September the **eighth** (September **8th**).

# eighty

*the number* 80
There are **eighty** pages in the book.

Fifty plus thirty equals **eighty** (50 + 30 = 80).
David went to France in nineteen **eighty**-four (1984).

# either

1 Michael hasn't got a camera. His sister hasn't got one **either**.
2 **either** … **or**
"Do you want a drink? You can have **either** tea **or** coffee." – "Tea, please."

# elbow

*a part of the body*
Peter has his **elbow** on the table.

elbow

# electric

We have an **electric** cooker in our kitchen. Helen's family has a gas cooker.

# electrician

Frank is studying to be an **electrician**. He is learning about machines that use electricity.

# electricity

Cars use petrol. Televisions use **electricity**.

# elephant

*a large grey animal*
**Elephants** live in Africa and India.

# eleven

*the number* 11
My sister is **eleven** years old.
Ten plus one equals **eleven** (10 + 1 = 11).

# eleventh

November is the **eleventh** month of the year.
Isabel's birthday is on June the **eleventh** (June **11th**).

# else

"I bought some oranges and bananas." – "What **else** did you buy?" – "Nothing. We don't need anything **else**."

# empty

*adjective* **emptier, emptiest**

1 The big glass has lemonade in it. The small glass has nothing in it. It is **empty**.

*verb* **empties, emptying, emptied, emptied**
2 *to make something empty*
Alan **emptied** a bag of sugar into a bowl.

# end

*noun*
1 The **end** of the cat's tail is white.
At the **end** of the lesson the teacher goes away.
*verb*
2 This lesson **ends** at ten o'clock. The next lesson starts at five past ten.

# ending

*things that happen at the end of a story or a film*
The beginning of the story was sad, but it had a happy **ending**.

# enemy

*plural* **enemies**
*a person or a country that is not a friend*
Those two countries are **enemies**. Their soldiers are fighting each other.

# engine

*a machine that makes things move*
My car goes very slowly. It needs a new **engine**.

# engineer

Simon is studying to be an **engineer**. He is learning how to make roads and railways.

# engineering

*the work of an engineer*
Simon is studying **engineering** at university.

# English

*noun*
**1** "Do you speak **English**?" – "Yes, we learned **English** at school."
*adjective*
**2** John comes from England. He is **English**.

# enjoy

**1** "Do you like football?" – "Yes, I really **enjoy** it. I **enjoy** playing football with my friends."
**2 to enjoy yourself**
"Did you **enjoy yourself** at the zoo yesterday?" – "Yes, I **enjoyed myself** very much."

# enjoyable

Helen enjoys her lessons at school. The lessons are very **enjoyable**.

# enormous

*very big*
The pyramids are **enormous**. They are bigger than most buildings.

# enough

"Have we got **enough** oranges?" – "No. We've only got one kilo of oranges, but we need three kilos. We haven't got **enough**."

# enter

**1** *to go into*
Peter opened the door and **entered** the shop.
**2** There is going to be a race at Tom's school. Tom likes running. He is going to **enter** the race.

# entrance

The people are going through the **entrance** to the football ground.

# envelope

Helen is putting the letter in an **envelope**.

# equal

*verb* **equalling, equalled, equalled**
**1** Five plus three **equals** eight (5 + 3 = 8).
*adjective*
**2** June has thirty days, and September has thirty days. June and September have an **equal** number of days.

# equator

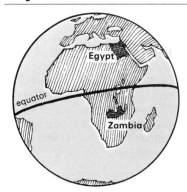

Egypt is north of the **equator**. Zambia is south of the **equator**.

# equipment

*things a person needs for a job*
A shoemaker needs the right **equipment** for making shoes.

# escape

**escaping, escaped, escaped**
*to get away*
The policeman caught the thief, but then the thief **escaped**.

# especially

It is very hot in Spain, **especially** in August. August is the hottest month of the year.

# etc.

*and other things*
You can buy a lot of things in the market. You can buy beans, tomatoes, onions, bananas, **etc.**

# even

**1** Not many cars have a telephone, but Robert's car has a telephone. It **even** has a television.
**2** This building is very big, but the new building will be **even** bigger.
**3 even if**
We will go to see my grandmother tomorrow, **even if** my father cannot come with us.

# evening

**1** *the last part of the day, before night*
Peter watches television in the **evening**, before he goes to bed.
**2 "Good evening."**
When you see someone in the evening you say, **"Good evening."**

# event

*something important that happens*
The Olympics is an **event** that happens every four years.

# ever

*at any time*
"Have you **ever** been to America?" – "No, I've never been there."

# every

All the girls in the class are from Madrid. **Every** girl in the class is from Madrid.

Martin gets up at six o'clock **every** day.

# everybody or everyone

*each person*
**Everybody** is at school today. They are all here.

# everything

*each thing*
Peter was in the shop. He looked at his list: "Sugar, eggs, bread ... yes, I've got all the things. I've got **everything**."

# everywhere

*in all places*
After the rain, there was water **everywhere**.

# exactly

There is no difference between those two cars. They are **exactly** the same.

# exam or examination

*an important test*
At the end of the year we have our school **exams**.

"Did you pass your English **exam**?" – "Yes. I got eighty per cent (80%)."

# example

**1** There are a lot of big towns in England. London and York are two **examples**.
**2 for example**
There are a lot of big towns in England – **for example**, London and York.

# except

All the boys are sitting on the floor, **except** one. One boy is standing.
Alan goes to school every day **except** Saturday and Sunday.

# excited

Paul likes animals very much. He is going to the zoo tomorrow. He's very **excited** about going to the zoo.

# exciting

The football match was very **exciting**! First England got a goal, then Spain, then England again, and a minute before the end Spain got another goal!

# exclamation mark

This is an **exclamation mark**    !
We sometimes use an **exclamation mark** when we write things that people say: "Peter, be quiet!"

# excuse me

Alan didn't have a watch. He said to a man in the street, "**Excuse me**, can you tell me the time?" – "Yes, it's three o'clock," the man said.
In the bus, a woman stepped on Tom's foot. "Oh, **excuse me!**" she said.

# exercise

**1** Tom gets a lot of **exercise**. He plays football and swims every day.
**2** "Do the **exercise** on page twenty-four of your books," said the teacher.
**3 exercise book**
The students wrote a story in their **exercise books**.

# exit

*a door out of a place*
This cinema is big. It has a lot of **exits**.

# expect

*to think that something is going to happen*
Michael didn't come to school today, but I **expect** he will come tomorrow.

## expensive

*costing a lot of money*
Cars aren't cheap. They are **expensive**.

## explain

*to help someone to understand something*
There were a lot of English words that I couldn't understand. The teacher **explained** them to me, and now I understand them.

## explanation

The teacher gave us an **explanation** of the difficult words. Then we understood them.

## extra

Most weeks we have two days holiday, but next week we have three days. There is an **extra** holiday next week.

## eye

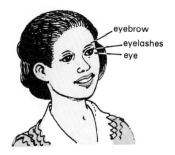

*a part of the face*
We see with our **eyes**.

## eyebrow

*the hair above the eyes*
Kate has black **eyebrows**.

## eyelash

*plural* **eyelashes**
*a hair on the part of the eye that closes*
Kate has long **eyelashes**.

# F f

## face

Your eyes, nose, and mouth are parts of your **face**.

## fact

**1** *something that is true*
It is a **fact** that the River Nile is 6670 kilometres long.
**2 in fact**
*really*
Andrew says he is not fat. **In fact** he is very fat.

## factory

*plural* **factories**
Many people work in a car **factory**. They make a lot of cars every week.

## fail

**1** *not to be able to do something*
Peter tried to swim across the river, but it was too difficult. He **failed**.
**2** *not to pass*
Helen was very sad when she **failed** her exams.

## fair

*not dark*
John's hair is **fair**. Paul's hair is dark.

## fairly

It is not difficult to make a kite. It is **fairly** difficult to make a chair. It is very difficult to make a clock.

## fall

*verb* **falling, fell, fallen**
**1** It is raining. The rain is **falling**.

The children were running. One of them **fell down**. Helen **fell off** her bicycle yesterday and cut herself.
**2 to fall asleep**
*to go to sleep*
Alan sometimes **falls asleep** when he watches television.
*noun*
**3** Helen fell off her bicycle. After her **fall**, she went to hospital.

## false

*not true*
"Is it true or **false** that the Amazon is the longest river in the world?" – "It's **false**. The Nile is the longest river."

## family

*plural* **families**

There are five people in Steven's **family**: Steven, his wife, and their three children.

# famous

William Shakespeare was a **famous** writer. Everyone knows his plays.

# fan

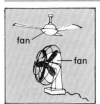

There is an electric **fan** in the classroom.

# fantastic

*very good*
The film was **fantastic**. We liked it very much.

# far

**1 farther, farthest** *or* **further, furthest**
"How **far** is the cinema from here?" – "It's not **far**. It's about a kilometre."
"Can we go to the sea on Saturday?" – "No. It's too **far away**."
**2 so far**
*to now*
Nick is reading a book about England. **So far**, he has read fifty pages.

# fare

*the money that you must pay when you go on a bus or train*
"What is the **fare** to the town on this bus?" – "It's ten pence."

# farm

Martin has a **farm**. He has a lot of animals and he grows many vegetables.

# farmer

Martin has a farm. He is a **farmer**.

# farther

"I'm tired. I can't walk any **farther**."
"Where is the shop?" – "Go past the school. **Farther on**, you will see the shop."
**Further** is another word for **farther**.

# farthest

"Who can swim the **farthest**, you or Nick?" – "I can swim farther than Nick."
**Furthest** is another word for **farthest**.

# fast

**1** *not slow*
Robert has a very **fast** car. His car can go at 150 kilometres per hour.
**2** *not slowly*
A lion can run **fast**. A donkey cannot run **fast**.

# fat

**fatter, fattest**

That man is **fat**. The woman is thin.

# father

Paul is the son of Steven and Jane. Steven is Paul's **father**.

# fault

*a mistake*
"Why did the little girl run into the road?" – "Because I didn't close the door. It was my **fault**."

# favourite

"What fruit do you like?" – "I like apples and oranges, but I like bananas best. Bananas are my **favourite** fruit."

# fear

*what you feel when you are afraid*
Kate saw a snake. She shook with **fear**.

# feather

*a part of the outside of a bird*
Birds have a lot of **feathers**.

# February

*the second month of the year*
There are twenty-eight days in **February**.

# fed

**1** *past and part of* **feed**
Nick **fed** the horse this morning. It doesn't need food now.
**2 fed up**
*not happy*
"I don't like working in this office. I'm **fed up** with this job."

# feed

**feeding, fed, fed**
*to give food to*
Nick **feeds** his dog every morning.

# feel

**feeling, felt, felt**
**1** *to be*
"Do you want something to eat?" – "Yes, I **feel** very hungry."
Nick's sister is going away. Nick **feels** very sad.
**2** Susan **felt** in her pocket for her key.

# feet

*plural of* **foot**
We wear shoes on our **feet**.

# fell

*past of* **fall**
Some apples **fell** from the tree to the ground.

# felt

*past and part of* **feel**
Kate **felt** happy when she saw her friends again.

# female

Jane is a woman. She is **female**. Steven is a man. He is male.

# fence

There is a **fence** round the field. The goats cannot eat the plants.

# ferry

*plural* **ferries**
*a boat that takes people across the sea or a river*
Tom went from England to France on the **ferry**.

# fetch

**fetches, fetching, fetched, fetched**
"We need some eggs," said Peter's mother. "Go and **fetch** some from the shop, Peter."

# few

*not many*
**1** Very **few** people in this village have cars. Most people have bicycles.
**2** There are a lot of students in the playground. There are only **a few** students inside.

# field

The men are working in the **field**.

# fifteen

*the number* **15**
Kate is **fifteen** years old.
Eight plus seven equals **fifteen** (8 + 7 = **15**).

# fifth

May is the **fifth** month of the year.
Tom's birthday is on the **fifth** of June (**5th** June).

# fifty

*the number* **50**
There were **fifty** eggs in the basket.
Twenty plus thirty equals **fifty** (20 + 30 = **50**).
There are **fifty**-two (52) weeks in a year.

# fig

*a green fruit*
There are some **figs** on the tree.

# fight

**fighting, fought, fought**

**1** The boys are **fighting**.
**2** A soldier **fights** for his country.

# figure

*a number*
1, 2, 3, 4, 5 are **figures**.
A, B, C, D, E are letters.

# fill

Nick is **filling** the bottle with water.

# film

We are going to the cinema tomorrow. We are going to see a **film**.

# final

*last*
My brother is in his **final** year at university. Next year he will start work.

# finally

*at last*
Robert drove for many hours. **Finally** he got to London.

# find

**finding, found, found**

1 David cannot **find** his car keys.

**2 to find out**
*to learn*
"How can I **find out** when the bus leaves?" – "Ask the driver. He will tell you."

# fine

1 *very good*
The weather is **fine** today. The sun is shining and there are no clouds.
2 *very well*
"How are you?" – "I'm **fine**, thanks!"

# finger

*a part of the hand*
Robert wears a ring on his **finger**.

# finish

**finishes, finishing, finished, finished**
The lesson started at nine o'clock and **finished** at ten o'clock.
Peter **finished** his homework, and then he watched television.

# fire

1 Jenny is sitting in front of the **fire**.

**Fire** is hot and can burn you.
2 There was a big **fire** in the factory.
**3 fire engine**
*a lorry that brings water when there is a fire*
When a building is burning, the **fire engine** comes quickly.

# first

1 January is the **first** month of the year.
Lisa's birthday is on the **first** of December (**1st** December).
2 "What did you do last night?" – "**First** I did my homework. Then I watched television."

# fish

*plural* **fish**
This man sells **fish** in the market.

# fisherman

*plural* **fishermen**
Andrew is a **fisherman**. He catches fish in the sea.

# fishing

*getting fish from a river or from the sea*
Paul likes **fishing**. He **goes fishing** every week. Sometimes he catches a big fish.

# fit

*verb* **fitting, fitted, fitted**
1 These shoes do not **fit** me. They are too big.
There are seven people in our family. We cannot all **fit** into our car.

*adjective* **fitter, fittest**
2 Nick is very **fit**. He keeps **fit** by running and playing football.

# five

*the number* **5**
We have **five** toes on each foot.
Four plus one equals **five** $(4 + 1 = 5)$.

# fix

**fixes, fixing, fixed, fixed**
The blackboard fell down. The teacher **fixed** it to the wall again.

# flag

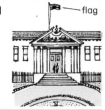

There is a **flag** on the roof of the building.

flag

# flat

*adjective* **flatter, flattest**

1 There are no hills near the river. The fields are very **flat**.

*noun*
2 Robert lives in a **flat**.
There are a lot of **flats** in this building. The building is called a **block of flats**.

# flavour

*a taste*
I like the **flavour** of this food.

# flew

*past of* **fly**
The bird **flew** back to its nest.

# flies

*verb*
**1** *part of* **fly**
Christopher **flies** to France every year.
*noun*
**2** *plural of* **fly**
There are some **flies** on the donkey's nose.

# flight

"When can I fly to Madrid, please?" – "There is a **flight** at six o'clock, and a **flight** at nine."

# float

Wood **floats** on water. Metals sink in water.

# flood

*noun*
**1** After the rain, there were **floods**. There was a lot of water on the fields near the river.
*verb*
**2** The river **flooded** the fields after the rain.
After the rain, the road was **flooded**. Cars could not use it.

# floor

**1** Peter is sitting on the **floor**.

**2** There are four **floors** in the block of flats. Robert lives on the third **floor**.

# flour

We make bread with **flour** and water.

# flower

These are **flowers**.

# flown

*part of* **fly**
"Where's that bird?" – "It has **flown** away."

# fly

*verb* **flies, flying, flew, flown**

**1** The bird is **flying** in the sky.

**2** Michael went on a plane last year. He **flew** from London to New York.
**3** The pilot **flew** the plane from London to Rome.
*noun, plural* **flies**

**4** There is a **fly** on the wall.

# fold

Susan is **folding** the letter.

# follow

*to go after*
The teacher went out and the students **followed** her.

# food

We eat **food** every day. Meat, vegetables, bread, and fruit are all kinds of **food**.

# foolish

*stupid*
There are a lot of cars on the road. Simon is going too fast in his car. He is very **foolish**.

# foot

*plural* **feet**
*a part of the body*
A **foot** has five toes.

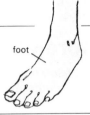

foot

# football

*a game for two teams that you play with a ball*
The boys are playing **football**.

# for

**1** There is a letter **for** Susan on the table.
**2** That knife is **for** cutting bread.
Our school is **for** girls.
**3** "Can I carry that box **for** you?" – "Thank you."
**4** Nick had meat and potatoes **for** dinner.
**5** Tom read **for** an hour.
**6** I bought this pen **for** fifty pence.

# forehead

forehead

*a part of the face*
This is Kate's **forehead**.

# foreign

*from another country*
Peter has a lot of **foreign** stamps. He has stamps from Australia, America, and many other countries.

# foreigner

*a person from another country*
John comes from England, but he lives in Paris. He is a **foreigner** in Paris.

# forest

There is a **forest** on the other side of the river.

# forget

**forgetting, forgot, forgotten**
*not to remember*
"Did you buy the meat?" – "No, I'm sorry, I **forgot**."

# fork

fork

Mark is eating with a **fork**.

# form

VISA FORM
Name: Helen Smith
Address: 16 High St
Bru...
Age:

1 Helen is writing her address on the **form**.
2 "Looked" is the past **form** of "look".

# fortnight

*two weeks*
"How long was your holiday in France?" – "A **fortnight**."

# forty

*the number* **40**
There are **forty** students in our class.
Twenty plus twenty equals **forty** ($20 + 20 = 40$).
There are only **forty**-three (43) boys in Paul's school.

# forward

**1 forward** *or* **forwards**
The traffic lights are green. The traffic is moving **forward**.
The lion walked **backwards and forwards** in its cage.
**2 to look forward to**
Helen is going to France for her holiday next week. She is very happy. She is **looking forward to** it very much.

# fought

*past and part of* **fight**
Two boys **fought** in the playground last week. The teacher was very angry.

# found

*past and part of* **find**
Peter could not find his pen. Tom **found** it under the desk.

# four

*the number* **4**
A square has **four** sides.
Three plus one equals **four** ($3 + 1 = 4$).

# fourteen

*the number* **14**
My sister is **fourteen** years old.
Ten plus four equals **fourteen** ($10 + 4 = 14$).

# fourth

April is the **fourth** month of the year.
Helen's birthday is on the **fourth** of July (**4th** July).

# fox

*plural* **foxes**

*an animal like a dog*
**Foxes** have long tails.

# free

*not costing any money*
Most schools in England are **free**. You do not pay to go to them.

# fresh

This bread is **fresh**. The baker made it only an hour ago.

# Friday

Today is **Friday**. Yesterday was Thursday. Tomorrow will be Saturday.
On **Fridays** Nick plays tennis.

# fridge

*a machine which makes food cold*
"Put the meat in the **fridge**. We can eat it tomorrow."

# fried

*past and part of* **fry**
Isabel **fried** an egg for her breakfast this morning.

# friend

Tom likes Peter. Peter likes Tom. They are good **friends**.

# friendly

**friendlier, friendliest**
Nick is a **friendly** person. He likes talking to other people and helping them.

# friendship

Steven and Christopher were friends at school, and they are friends now. Their **friendship** has lasted many years.

# fries

*part of* **fry**
Isabel **fries** an egg for her breakfast every morning.

# frightened

*afraid*
Kate was **frightened** when she saw a snake.

# frog

*a small animal*
There is a **frog** on the leaves.

# from

1 This bus goes **from** London to Bristol.
Martin works **from** nine o'clock in the morning to five o'clock in the afternoon.
2 Our house is two kilometres **from** the village.
3 The teacher took some books **from** the cupboard.
4 This letter is **from** my uncle. We buy vegetables **from** the greengrocer's.
5 The baker makes bread **from** flour.

# front

1 The teacher is at the **front** of the classroom. Susan is sitting at the back.
2 Steven and his wife sit in the **front** seat of the car. The children sit in the back seat.

**3 in front of**
There is a tree **in front of** our house.

# fruit

*the soft sweet part of a plant or a tree that you can eat*
"What **fruit** do you like?" – "I like apples, bananas, and oranges."

# fry

**fries, frying, fried, fried**
*to cook something in oil*
Maria is **frying** some fish. She is going to eat it for dinner.

# frying pan

Martin is cooking some eggs. The eggs are in the **frying pan**.

# full

The big glass is **full** of lemonade. The small glass is empty.

# full stop

This is a **full stop**
We write a **full stop** at the end of a sentence.

# fun

The children are laughing and playing. They are having **fun**.

# funny

**funnier, funniest**
1 The film was very **funny**. We all laughed a lot.
2 *strange*
"Where's my book? I left it on this table yesterday, but now it isn't there. That's **funny**!"

# furniture

There is a lot of **furniture** in this room. There are tables, chairs, lamps, a desk, and a television.

# further

"I'm tired. I can't walk any **further**."

**Farther** is another word for **further**.

# furthest

"Who can jump the **furthest**, you or Peter?" – "I can jump further than Peter."

**Farthest** is another word for **furthest**.

# future

**1** In the **future**, people may live on the moon.
**2** "Will see" is the **future** tense of "see".
**3 in future**
"You're late again," the teacher said. "**In future**, come to school at the right time."

# G g

# game

**1** My sister is playing a **game**. She is playing with her friends.
**2** "Would you like a **game** of chess?" – "Yes, let's play chess."

# garage

**1** Robert is at the **garage**.

**2** *a small building where you put a car*
Christopher is putting his car in the **garage**.

# garden

Mark is reading the newspaper in his **garden**.

# garlic

*a vegetable*
Robert doesn't like **garlic** in his food.

# gas

**1** *plural* **gases**
Air is a **gas**. Water is a liquid. Air is made of different **gases**.
**2** We use **gas** when we cook our food.
We can get **gas** from a **gas cylinder**.

# gate

This man is closing the school **gates**.

# gave

*past of* **give**
Maria **gave** her mother a present yesterday.

# geese

*plural of* **goose**
There are some **geese** on our farm.

# gentleman

*plural* **gentlemen**
Robert's grandfather is a kind old **gentleman**.

# geography

In the **geography** lesson Nick learned about the rivers and mountains of England.

# get

**getting, got, got**
**1** Maria **gets** some eggs from the market every week.
**2** Nick **got** a letter from his uncle today.
"Did Christopher **get** the books?" – "Yes, a boy brought them this morning."
**3** That young plant is **getting** bigger every day.
Tom played football all afternoon. He **got** very tired.
**4 to get to**
*to come to a place*
The train left London at two o'clock and **got to** Bristol at six o'clock.

**5 to get up**
Paul is **getting up**.

**6 to get in**
Jane opened the door of the car and **got in**.

**7 to get out**
Robert stopped the car and **got out**.
**8 to get on**
The bus came, and Alan **got on**.
**9 to get off**
The train stopped in London. Everyone **got off**.
**10 to get away**
The police caught the thief, but then the thief **got away**. He climbed out of a window.

# ghost

*the shape of a dead person that some people think you can see*
Some people say that they have seen the **ghost** of a lady who died hundreds of years ago.

# giraffe

*a very tall animal*
**Giraffes** have long necks.

# girl

Lisa is a **girl**. Peter and Paul are boys.

# give

**giving, gave, given**

Helen is **giving** her book to the teacher. The teacher is taking the book.
My uncle **gave** me a new bicycle today.

# glad

*happy*
The holidays start today. The students are very **glad**.

# glass

**1** Martin is putting some new **glass** in the window.

**2** *plural* **glasses**
Susan is drinking some water from a **glass**.

# glasses

glasses

Alice cannot see very well. She must wear **glasses**.

# glove

This is a pair of **gloves**.

# glue

Alice has broken a plate. She is using **glue** to put the pieces together.

# go

**goes, going, went, gone**
**1** Steven **goes** to the town in the morning. He **goes** to his office. At four o'clock he **goes home**.
**2** Peter **goes** shopping every afternoon. Then he **goes** swimming with his friends.
**3 to go for**
It was a very nice day. Mark **went for** a walk beside the river.
**4 to go back**
This morning Maria bought some eggs in a shop, but she didn't put them in her bag. This afternoon she **went back** to get them.
**5 to go on**
The students are reading. The teacher says, "**Go on** reading. You can stop at twelve o'clock."

# goal

The ball is going into the **goal**.

# goat

*an animal*
There is a **goat** in the field.

# goes

*part of* **go**
Alan **goes** to school every day.

# going

*part of* **go**
"Where are you **going**?" – "I'm **going** to the station."

# going to

"Did you do that work today?" – "No, I didn't. I am **going to** do it tomorrow."
There are a lot of clouds in the sky. It is **going to** rain.

# gold

*noun*
**1** *a yellow metal*
**Gold** costs a lot of money.
**2** *the colour of this metal*
**Gold** is a very nice colour.
*adjective*
**3** "What colour is your car?" – "It's **gold**."

# gone

*part of* **go**
Christopher is not here. He has **gone** to London. He is still there.

# good

**better, best**
**1** We had a **good** holiday. We saw a lot of places.
**2 good at**
Tom is **good at** geography. He is going to study geography at university.
**3 good for**
Fruit and vegetables are **good for** you, but sweets are bad for you.
**4** "Good morning."
Before the first lesson, the teacher says "**Good morning**" to the students.

# goodbye

"I must go now. **Goodbye**." – "**Goodbye**, Peter."

# goodnight

"I'm going to bed now," said Lisa. "**Goodnight**, mother." – "**Goodnight**, Lisa."

# goose

*plural* **geese**

*a large bird*
This is a **goose**.

# got

**1** *past and part of* **get**
Anne **got** some vegetables from the market yesterday.
**2 to have got**
*to have*
Peter **has got** a bicycle.
"**Have** you **got** a watch?" – "Yes, I have."

# government

*the people who decide what happens in a country*
The **government** pays for new roads, schools, and hospitals.

# gram or gramme

*a measurement of weight*
There are a thousand **grams** in a kilogram (1000g = 1kg).

"How much does this letter weigh, please?" – "It weighs twenty **grams** (20g)."

# grandchild

*plural* **grandchildren**
*the child of your child*
Anne has three **grandchildren**: Lisa, Paul, and Peter.

# granddaughter

*the daughter of your child*

## grandfather or grandpa

*the father of your father or your mother*

## grandmother or grandma

*the mother of your father or your mother*

## grandparent

*the mother or the father of your mother or your father*
Steven's grandfather died last week. Now he has only got three **grandparents**.

## grandson

*the son of your child*

## grape

*a small round fruit*
**Grapes** are green or black.

## grapefruit

*plural* **grapefruit**
*a large yellow fruit*
A **grapefruit** is bigger than an orange.

## grass

There is a lot of **grass** near the river.
Horses and cows eat **grass**.

## great

*big and important*
The River Nile is one of the **great** rivers of the world.

## greedy

**greedier, greediest**
Maria has eaten all the bananas. She is very **greedy**.

## green

*the colour of grass*
*noun*
1 We make **green** when we put blue and yellow together.
*adjective*
2 Peter likes his **green** shirt.

## greengrocer

A **greengrocer** sells fruit and vegetables.
Isabel bought some onions, carrots, and bananas at the **greengrocer's**.

## grew

*past of* **grow**
Last year David **grew** a lot of vegetables in his garden.

## grey

*the colour of elephants*
*noun*
1 We make **grey** when we put black and white together.
*adjective*
2 The sky is very **grey** today.

## grocer

A **grocer** sells sugar, eggs, coffee, and many other things.
Robert wants to buy some coffee. He is going to the **grocer's**.

## ground

1 Nick is sitting in the tree. Maria is standing on the **ground**.

2 The football **ground** is between the school and the river. We play football there every day.

## group

A **group** of boys is standing. Another **group** is sitting on the ground.

## grow

**growing, grew, grown**
1 A lot of trees **grow** near the river.
2 Martin **grows** vegetables and fruit on his farm.
**3 to grow up**
Nick is **growing up**. Next year he will be as big as his father.

## grown-up

*adjective*
1 Maria is fourteen years old. She has two **grown-up** brothers: William is twenty, and Robert is twenty-two.
*noun*
2 There were a lot of children and some **grown-ups** in the cinema.

# guess

**guesses, guessing, guessed, guessed**
"**Guess** how old I am," said the little girl. "I don't know … Twelve years old?" – "No, I'm only ten."

# guide

*a person who shows places to you*
The **guide** took us around the castle and told us about it.

# guitar

Jenny is playing a **guitar**.

# gun

This soldier has two **guns**.

gun
gun

# Hh

# had

*past and part of* **have**
Maria **had** breakfast at seven o'clock today.
Michael has **had** a lot of coffee today.

# hadn't

*had not*
I saw my Uncle Frank today. I **hadn't** seen him for many years.

# had to

*past and part of* **have to**
Christopher went to France today. The plane left at 8.00. He **had to** get up very early.

# hair

Alan has short **hair**. His sister has very long **hair**.

# hairdresser

*a person who cuts hair*
The **hairdresser** is cutting Jenny's hair.
Jenny is at the **hairdresser's**.

# half

**1** *plural* **halves**
"**Half** (½) of the banana is for you, and **half** is for me."

**2** "What's the time?" – "It's **half** past two (2.30)."

# hall

*a very large room*
All the students in our school are in the **hall**. They are listening to the teacher.

# halves

*plural of* **half**
Jane cut the oranges into **halves**.

# hamburger

*a round piece of meat inside a piece of bread*
Jenny likes eating **hamburgers**.

# hammer

Martin is making a table. He is using a **hammer**.

# hand

**1** *a part of the body*
A **hand** has five fingers.

Susan is holding a pen in her **hand**.
**2** A clock has two **hands**.

# handkerchief

Jenny is holding a **handkerchief**.

# handle

*the part of something that you hold*
Lisa is turning the **handle** of the door.

# handsome

**handsomer, handsomest**
*nice to look at*
That actor is very **handsome**.

# hang

**hanging, hung, hung**
1 Apples **hung** from every branch of the tree.

**2 to hang up**
Christopher is **hanging** his coat **up**.

# happen

"We laughed a lot in the class yesterday." – "Why? What **happened**?" – " A cat came into the classroom."

# happily

The children are watching the puppets. They are happy. They are laughing **happily**.

# happy

**happier, happiest**
Susan is very **happy**. She is laughing.

# harbour

All the fishing boats are in the **harbour** today. There is so much wind and rain that they cannot go out to sea.

# hard

1 *not soft*
This metal is very **hard**. I cannot cut it.
2 *difficult*
The teacher asked us a very **hard** question. We could not answer it.
3 *a lot*
My father works very **hard**. He works for ten hours every day.

# hardly

The box is very big. Tom can **hardly** carry it.

# harvest

*the bringing in of fruit and vegetables from the fields*
The **harvest** was good this year. There are a lot of vegetables in the shops.

# has

*part of* **have**
Jane **has** black hair.
Peter **has** a bicycle. He **has got** a bicycle.
Helen **has** lunch at two o'clock.
Susan **has** done the exercise.

# hasn't

*has not*
Tom **hasn't** got a watch.

# has to

*part of* **have to**
*must*
The bus does not go to the school. Kate **has to** walk to school.

# hat

Bill is wearing a **hat**.

hat

# hate

**hating, hated, hated**
"Do you like onions?" – "No, I **hate** them. I never eat onions."

# have

**has, having, had, had**
1 My father **has** brown eyes. I don't **have** brown eyes.
My father **has got** brown eyes. I **haven't got** brown eyes.
2 Lisa **has** breakfast at eight o'clock every morning.
3 The students **have** an English lesson on Tuesdays.
4 "**Have** you been to America?" – "Yes, I **have**."

# haven't

*have not*
My young brothers **haven't** started to learn French.

# have to

**has to, having to, had to, had to**
*must*
We **have to** get up at eight o'clock. School starts at nine o'clock.

# he

"Where is Nick?" – "**He** is outside. **He** is sitting in the car."

# head

*a part of the body*
Alice is wearing a hat on her **head**.

# headache

Maria is ill.
She has got a
**headache**.

# headmaster

*a man who is the most
important teacher in a school*
Mr Smith is the **headmaster** of
our school. His office is in the
school.

# headmistress

*plural* **headmistresses**
*a woman who is the most
important teacher in a school*
Mrs Brown is the **headmistress**
of our school. Her office is in
the school.

# health

*how well your body is*
Walking and running are good
for your **health**.

# hear

**hearing, heard, heard**
1 "Listen! Can you **hear**
anything?" – "Yes, I can **hear**
a bell. I can **hear** it ringing."
2 *to get news of something*
"Louise has a new baby." –
"Yes, I know. I **heard**
yesterday."
"Have you **heard from** your
brother?" – "Yes, I have. I got
a letter from him yesterday."

# heart

*a part of the body*
The **heart** makes blood go
round the body.

# heat

*noun*
1 The sun is hot. It gives us
**heat**.

*verb*
2 *to make something hot*
Louise is **heating** some soup.

# heavy

**heavier,
heaviest**
Tom cannot
carry the box.
The box is very
**heavy**.

# hectare

*a measurement of land*
"How big is this field?" – "It is
half a **hectare**."
Martin has a farm of four
**hectares** (4**ha**).

# he'd

1 *he would*
Nick said **he'd** go to the cafe,
but he didn't.
2 *he had*
I went to see Peter, but **he'd**
gone to school.

# hedge

hedge

There is a **hedge** between the
field and the river.

# height

"What is the **height** of this
building?" – "It is fifteen
metres high."

# held

*past of* **hold**
Alan **held** the bird in his hand.

# helicopter

Frank is flying in a **helicopter**.

# he'll

*he will*
Tom is at school today, but
**he'll** be at home tomorrow.

# hello

Nick saw his friend in the
street. "**Hello!**" he said.
Christopher picked up the
telephone. "**Hello!**" he said.

# help

*noun*
1 Jenny cannot carry her bag.
She needs some **help**.
*verb*
2 Jenny cannot carry her bag.
Helen is **helping** her.

**3 "Help yourself."**
*"Please take it."*
"Please can I have one of your bananas?" – "Yes, of course. **Help yourself**."

## helpful

"I can't do this exercise." – "Nick will help you. He is very **helpful**."

## hen

*a bird*
We get eggs from **hens**.

## her

1 "Where is Maria? I can't see **her**."
Susan went to the shops, and we went with **her**.
2 Lisa is reading **her** book.

## here

1 "Put the books **here**, please."
"**Here** is a present for you. Please take it."
2 "**Here comes** …"
"Sit down everybody! **Here comes** the teacher!"
3 "**Here you are.**"
"Please give me that newspaper." – "**Here you are.**" – "Thank you."

## hers

This is Lisa's book. The book is **hers**.

## herself

1 The little girl hurt **herself** when she fell down.
2 *without any help*
Helen made this dress **herself**.
3 **by herself**
*without any other person*
Susan went to school **by herself** yesterday.

## he's

1 *he is*
Nick is a boy. **He's** a big boy.
2 *he has*
Tom is happy. **He's** got a new bicycle.

## Hi!

Kate saw her friend in the street. "**Hi!**" she said.
**Hello!** is another word for **Hi!** but you only say **Hi!** to your friends.

## hide

**hiding, hid, hidden**

1 Michael cannot find his young sister. She is **hiding** under the table.
2 Peter **hid** Tom's pen. Tom could not find it.

## high

1 The plane is flying **high** in the sky.
2 There is a very **high** wall behind our house. I cannot see over it.
3 "How **high** is the hill?" – "It is a hundred metres **high**."

## hill

A car is going up the **hill**.

## him

"Where is Nick?" – "He is in the garden. I can see **him**."
Tom went to the cafe. His friend went with **him**.

## himself

1 Nick is looking at **himself**.

2 *without any help*
Michael made this table **himself**.
3 **by himself**
*without any other person*
Tom walks to school **by himself** every day.

## hippo or hippopotamus

*plural* **hippos** *or* **hippopotamuses**
*a large animal*
There are some **hippos** in the river.

# his

1 Robert is sitting in **his** car.
2 This is Robert's car. The car is **his**.

# history

In **history** lessons we learn about the past. This week we learned about Napoleon.

# hit

**hitting, hit, hit**
The lorry is **hitting** the tree.

# hobby

*plural* **hobbies**
*something that you like to do when you are not working*
Maria has a camera. She likes taking photos. It is her **hobby**.

# hockey

*a game for two teams that you play with sticks and a small ball*
The boys are playing **hockey**.

# hold

**holding, held, held**
1 *to have in your hand*
Maria is **holding** a bottle.

Bill **held on to** his hat because it was very windy.
2 This bottle **holds** one litre. You can put a litre of water in it.

# hole

The men are making a **hole** in the road.
Alan has a **hole** in his shirt.

# holiday

Tomorrow is a **holiday**. No one will go to school tomorrow.
I am going to America for three weeks for my summer **holiday**.

# home

1 James studies in London, but his **home** is in Bristol.
2 **to go home**
At two o'clock, the students **go home** from school.

# home economics

*a school subject*
In the **home economics** lesson, Maria learns about cooking and making clothes.

# homework

I can't go to Lisa's house this evening. I must do my **homework**. The teacher will look at the **homework** tomorrow.

# honest

The shopkeeper was **honest**. I gave him too much money, but he ran after me and gave some money back to me.

# honey

*a sweet food that bees make*
Nick eats bread and **honey** for breakfast.

# hook

The butcher is putting the meat on a **hook**.

# hop

**hopping, hopped, hopped**

*to move on only one foot*
The girls are **hopping** on the grass.

# hope

**hoping, hoped, hoped**
*to want something to happen*
Helen is going to live in London. I **hope** she will be happy there.

# horn

1 This animal has two **horns**.

2 There is a dog on the road in front of Robert's car. Robert wants the dog to move. He is using his car **horn**.

# horrible

*making you afraid*
The children saw a big snake in the zoo. It was **horrible**. They were very afraid.

# horse

*a large animal*
The **horse** is eating some grass.

# hospital

Jane is a nurse. She works in a **hospital**.
Tom is very ill. He is **in hospital**.

# hot

**hotter, hottest**
1 The weather is **hot** in Spain. It is cold in England.
Peter is **hot**. He wants an ice cream.
2 This food is very **hot**. There is a lot of pepper in it. I cannot eat it.

# hot dog

*a piece of meat with bread round it*
Kate likes eating **hot dogs**.

# hotel

David is going into a **hotel**. He will sleep in the **hotel**.

# hour

*a part of a day*
There are sixty minutes in an **hour**.
There are twenty-four **hours** in a day.

# house

Lisa's family live in this **house**.

# how

1 "**How** do you come to school?" – "I come by bus."
2 "**How** heavy is that box?" – "It weighs ten kilos."
3 "**How old** is Lisa?" – "She is thirteen years old."
4 "**How many** oranges did you buy?" – "Five."
5 "**How much** sugar did you buy?" – "One kilo."
6 "**How much** is this pen?" – "Sixty pence."
7 "**How are you?**"
"**How are you?**" – "Very well, thank you."

# however

Nick goes to school every day. **However**, yesterday he did not go to school. It was a holiday.

# hundred

*the number* 100
There are a **hundred** and seventy people in our school.
Sixty plus forty equals one **hundred** ($60 + 40 = 100$).
There are **hundreds of** trees near the river.

# hung

*past of* **hang**
The teacher **hung** the pictures on the wall.

# hungry

**hungrier, hungriest**
Nick is very **hungry**. He didn't have breakfast or lunch today.

# hunt

Frank is **hunting** rabbits. He wants to eat one for dinner.

# hunter

Frank is a **hunter**. He hunts birds and animals with a gun.

# hurry

**hurries, hurrying, hurried, hurried**
1 *to go somewhere fast*
The boys are **hurrying** for the bus. They are late for school.
2 "**Hurry up!**"
"We're late for school, Nick. **Hurry up!**"
3 **in a hurry**
The boys are **in a hurry**. They are late for school.

# hurt

**hurting, hurt, hurt**
1 The little girl fell down and **hurt** her leg.
2 **to hurt yourself**
The little girl **hurt herself** when she fell down.

## husband

Steven and Jane are married. Steven is Jane's **husband**. Jane is Steven's wife.

# I i

## I

"What's your name?" – "I am Nick. My sister is called Maria."

## ice

*very cold water that is hard*
In the winter in cold countries there is **ice** on some rivers.

## ice cream

Paul likes eating **ice cream**.

## I'd

**1** *I would*
"Do you want a drink?" – "Yes, please, **I'd** like a cup of coffee."

**2** *I had*
"When you came to see me yesterday, **I'd** gone to the shops."

## idea

*something that you think*
"I've got an **idea**! Let's go and see Uncle Steven tomorrow!" – "Yes, that's a good **idea**."

## if

**1 If** it is cold, Peter eats in his house. **If** it is very hot, he eats outside.
**2** *whether*
I don't know **if** there are any snakes in England.

## I'll

*I will*
"**I'll** come and see you tomorrow."

## ill

Tom is **ill**. He is in bed. The doctor is looking at him.

## illness

*plural* **illnesses**
*being ill*
Helen was in hospital for a long time because of her **illness**, but now she is at school again.

## I'm

*I am*
"**I'm** Nick, and this is my sister, Maria."

## imagine

**imagining, imagined, imagined**
*to have a picture of something in your mind*
We **imagined** living a hundred years ago.

## immediately

*without waiting*
Nick heard the bell. He ran out of the classroom **immediately**.

## important

**1** A king is a very **important** man.
**2** When you are ill, it is **important** to do everything the doctor tells you to do.

## impossible

*that cannot happen*
"Those two men flew to the sun." – "That's **impossible**!"

## in

**1** Nick and David are **in** the car.
Simon lives **in** France. John lives **in** England.
**2 In** the summer, we do not go to school. We have a long holiday.
**3** Now it is five to one. The next lesson is **in** five minutes, at one o'clock.
**4** We speak to our English teacher **in** English.

## indoors

*in a building*
We eat **indoors** when it is cold. When it is hot, we sometimes eat outside.

# information

*things that you want to know*
"Can you give me some **information** about planes for London?" – "Yes. There's a plane at 6.00 and another one at 10.00."

# ink

The man is writing. He is using a pen and some **ink**.

# insect

*a very small animal with six legs*
Ants and bees are **insects**.

# inside

**1** When it is cold we eat **inside** the house. When it is hot, we sometimes eat outside the house.
**2** The **inside** of a watermelon is red. The outside is green.

# instead

*in the place of someone or something*
I didn't have a pen when I wrote the exercise. I used a pencil **instead**. I used a pencil **instead of** a pen.

# instructions

*words that tell you how to do something*
"How do I use this machine?" – "I don't know. Read the **instructions**. They will tell you what to do."

# interest

Peter likes football, but he has no **interest** in basketball.

# interested

*wanting to know more about something*
I am **interested** in animals. I am reading a book about them.

# interesting

Animals are very **interesting**. I like reading about them, and I want to know more about them.

# international

*of or for many countries*
There is an **international** airport in London. You can fly from London to many different countries.

# interrupt

*to say something when another person is speaking*
You must not **interrupt** the teacher.

# interview

Marlon Brando had an **interview** on television. He answered questions about his work.
Martin wants a new job. He will have an **interview** for the job tomorrow.

# into

Some people are going **into** the station.

# introduce

**introducing, introduced, introduced**
*to bring new people together and say their names*
Helen is **introducing** Lisa to her father: "Lisa, this is my father. Father, this is Lisa."

# invent

*to think of and make something new*
Alexander Graham Bell **invented** the telephone in 1876.

# invention

*thinking of and making something new*
Since the **invention** of television, we know more about other countries.

# inventor

*someone who thinks of and makes something new*
Alexander Graham Bell was the **inventor** of the telephone.

# invitation

*asking someone to come somewhere or to do something with you*
"Thank you for your **invitation**, but I can't come to dinner tomorrow. I'm sorry."

# invite

**inviting, invited, invited**
*to ask someone to come somewhere or to do something with you*
David **invited** Frank to dinner at his house.

# iron

*noun*
**1** *a strong metal*
The school gate is made of **iron**.

**2** *a thing that you make hot and then use to make clothes flat*
Alice is using an **iron**.

*verb*
**3** *to make clothes flat with an iron*
Alice is **ironing** a shirt.

## irregular

"Walk" (walking, walked, walked) is a regular verb.
"See" (seeing, saw, seen) is an **irregular** verb.

## is

*part of* **be**
George **is** an old man.
**Is** your sister a student?
This **is** my pencil.
Nick **is** writing a letter.

## island

*a piece of land with water round it*
There is an **island** in the middle of the river.

## isn't

*is not*
"Is Andrew a farmer?" – "No, he **isn't**. He's a shopkeeper."

## it

**1** There is a cat on the wall. **It** is a black cat.
"Where is my book? I can't find it."
**2** Yesterday **it** was raining, but today **it** is very hot.
**It** is Thursday today.

## it'll

*it will*
"I think **it'll** be sunny tomorrow."

## it's

**1** *it is*
"Where's the book?" – "**It's** on the table."
**2** *it has*
Steven's house is big. **It's** got seven rooms.

## its

The dog ate **its** food.

## itself

The cat is washing **itself**.

## I've

*I have*
**I've** got a new bicycle.

# J j

## jacket

Alan is wearing a **jacket**.

jacket

## jam

Jenny is putting some **jam** on her bread.

## January

*the first month of the year*
There are thirty-one days in **January**.

## jar

*something that you can put food in*
There is some rice in this **jar**.

## jeans

*trousers made from thick blue cotton*
Jenny is wearing **jeans**.

# jewel

*a stone that costs a lot of money*
These are **jewels**.

# job

"What's your **job**?" – "I'm a nurse. I work in a hospital."

# join

**1** *to put together*
Peter is **joining** the two pieces of the table.

**2** *to come together*
This small road **joins** a big road near my school.

# joke

*something that makes people laugh*
We laughed when Peter told us a **joke**.

# journey

*going from one place to a different place*
"How long is the **journey** from London to Bristol?" – "It's a three hour **journey** by car."

# judge

*a person who says what is right and what is wrong*
"That's my horse!" said George. "No, it's my horse!" said Frank. They went to the **judge**. The **judge** said it was George's horse.

# jug

Nick is putting some water in the **jug**.

# juice

*the liquid that comes from fruit and vegetables*
Lisa is drinking a glass of orange **juice**.

# July

*the seventh month of the year*
There are thirty-one days in **July**.

# jump

The cat is **jumping** down from the wall.

# June

*the sixth month of the year*
There are thirty days in **June**.

# jungle

*a place with a lot of trees and plants in hot countries*
You can see many different plants and animals in the **jungle**.

# just

**1** *a very short time ago*
"Where's my banana?" – "I've **just** eaten it."

**2** *a little*
This boy is **just** over one and a half metres tall. His sister is **just** under one and a half metres tall.
**3** Alan is **just** like his father. Everyone can see that they are from the same family.
**4** "Where is the cinema?" – "**Just** go along the street and you will see it."
"Are you coming with us, Helen?" – "**Just a minute!** I'm putting my coat on."

# K k

# keep

**keeping, kept, kept**
**1** Maria **keeps** her clothes in a cupboard in her bedroom.
**2** Everyone in the classroom was talking. "**Keep** quiet!" said the teacher. "Don't talk!"

# kept

*past and part of* **keep**
My grandfather has **kept** his old school books.

# kettle

We use a **kettle** when we need hot water.

# key

We open doors with **keys**.

# kick

*to hit something with your foot*
Peter is **kicking** the ball.

# kill

Lions **kill** other animals for food.

# kilo or kilogram

*a measurement of weight*
A **kilo** is one thousand grams
(**1kg** = 1000g).
Tom weighs fifty **kilos**.

# kilometre

*a measurement of length*
One **kilometre** equals one thousand metres
(**1km** = 1000m).
The school is two **kilometres** from my house.

# kind

*noun*
**1** "What **kind** of fruit did you buy?" – "I bought bananas, oranges, and apples."
*adjective*
**2** Lisa is a very **kind** person. She is carrying that old woman's basket for her.

# king

*a man who is the ruler of a country*
**King** Juan Carlos is the **King** of Spain.
The wife of a **king** is called a queen.

# kitchen

*a room in a house*
Martin is in the **kitchen**. He is cooking the lunch.

# kite

Peter is flying a **kite**.

# kitten

*a young cat*
That cat has two **kittens**.

# knee

*a part of the body*
Peter fell down. He cut his **knee**.

# knew

*past of* **know**
I **knew** your grandfather very well.

# knife

*plural* **knives**
David is cutting the bread with a **knife**.

# knock

**1** David is **knocking** at the door.

**2 to knock down**
The lorry hit a tree. It **knocked** the tree **down**.

# knot

There is a **knot** in the string.

knot

# know

**knowing, knew, known**
**1** "Do you **know** the answer to this question?"
**2** "Do you **know** my brother?"
– "I've spoken to him a few times, but I don't **know** him very well."

# Ll

## label

"This is my bag. There is a **label** on it."

These things have **labels** on them.

## ladder

Jenny is painting the wall. She is standing on a **ladder**.

## lady

*plural* **ladies**
*a woman*
Robert's grandmother is an old **lady**.

## laid

*past and part of* **lay**
Our hen **laid** two eggs yesterday.

## lain

*part of* **lie**
That cat has **lain** in our garden every day this week.

## lake

*a big piece of water with land around it*
**Lake** Windermere is a big **lake** in England.

## lamb

**1** *a young sheep*
We saw some **lambs** in the field.
**2** *the meat of a young sheep*
We had some **lamb** and vegetables for dinner yesterday.

## lamp

There is a **lamp** on the table.

## land

*noun*
**1** Animals live on the **land**. Fish live in the sea.
*verb*
**2** *to come down to the ground*
Christopher went to London by plane. The plane **landed** at London Airport.

## language

"David, what **languages** do you speak?" – "I speak Spanish, and English, and French."

## large

**larger, largest**
*not small*
Elephants are **large** animals. Cats are small animals.

## last

**1** The first letter of the alphabet is "A". The **last** letter is "Z".
**2** Michael went to the cinema **last** week. This week he will go to the theatre.
**3** The lesson starts at nine o'clock. It ends at ten o'clock. The lesson **lasts** one hour.
**4 at last**
*after a very long time*
We waited a long time, and **at last** the bus came.

## late

**later, latest**
**1** *after the right time*
School starts at 9.00, but Maria came at 9.15 today. She was fifteen minutes **late**.
Maria was **late for** school.
**2** *near the end of the day*
Michael gets up early in the morning, and he goes to bed **late** at night.

# later

*after some time*
Yesterday afternoon we played football. **Later**, we went to a cafe.

# latest

Nick is listening to the radio. He is listening to the **latest** news.

# laugh

The children are happy. They are **laughing**.

# law

*what the government says you must do or must not do*
The **law** says that we must not drive too fast.

# lawyer

*someone who helps you with the law*
Kate's brother studied for five years at London University to become a **lawyer**.

# lay

**1** *verb* **laying, laid, laid**
Birds **lay** eggs. The eggs come from the body of the bird.
**2** *past of the verb* **lie**
Tom **lay** on his bed for an hour.

# lazy

**lazier, laziest**
Frank doesn't like work. He doesn't do his work. He is **lazy**.

# lead

**leading, led, led**
*to take a person, or sometimes an animal, to a place*
I asked a man where the station was. The man **led** me to it.

# leader

We are playing a game. Tom is the **leader**. Tom tells us what we must do.

# leaf

*plural* **leaves**

—leaf

Trees and plants have **leaves**. **Leaves** are green.

# lean

**leaning, leant** *or* **leaned, leant** *or* **leaned**

 Peter is **leaning** against a tree.

# learn

**learning, learned** *or* **learnt, learned** *or* **learnt**
Babies **learn** how to talk.
Tom studies geography at school. Yesterday he **learned** the names of all the rivers in America.

# least

**1** Tom has 80 pence. Nick has 60 pence. Peter has 50 pence. Peter has **the least** money.
**2 at least**
*not less than*
"How many people work in that big shop?" – "**At least** twenty people."

# leather

*noun*
**1** *the skin of an animal*
Shoes and bags are sometimes made of **leather**.
*adjective*
**2** *made of the skin of an animal*
Nick wears a **leather** belt.

# leave

**leaving, left, left**
**1** *to go away*
Christopher goes to his office every day. He **leaves** his house at eight o'clock in the morning.
**2** *not to take something with you*
"Where are the car keys?" – "I've **left** them on the table in the kitchen."
**3** *not to take something*
"Can I have this cake, mother?" – "No, **leave** it. It's for Lisa."

# leaves

*plural of* **leaf**
There are a lot of **leaves** on the tree.

# led

*past and part of* **lead**
The farmer **led** his cows to the market.

# left

**1** Most people write with their right hand, not with their **left** hand.

**2** The shops are on the **left** of the street. They are on the **left-hand side** of the street. The school is on the right.
**3** *past and part of* **leave**
The train **left** the station at ten o'clock this morning.

# leg

*a part of the body*
A cat has four **legs**. A bird has two **legs**.

# lemon

*a yellow fruit*
There are a lot of **lemons** on our tree.

# lemonade

*a drink*
We make **lemonade** with lemons, sugar, and water.

# lend

**lending, lent, lent**

*to give something to someone for a short time*
"I haven't got a pen." – "Here, I'll **lend** you my pen."

# length

This table is two metres long. The **length** of this table is two metres.

# lent

*past and part of* **lend**
My sister **lent** me her camera when I went to America.

# leopard

*a large animal*
**Leopards** are yellow and black.

# less

**1** A bicycle costs **less** than a car.
**2** Bicycles are **less** expensive than cars.
**3** A car needs **less** petrol than a bus.

# lesson

The students are having an English **lesson**.

# let

**letting, let, let**
**1** Our teacher does not **let** us talk in class.
**2** "**Let's** …"
"Shall we go to the cinema?" – "No. **Let's** watch the football on television." – "Yes, let's."

**3 to let in**
"Steven, please open the door and **let** the children **in**."

# letter

**1** A, B, C, D, E, and F are **letters**. There are twenty-six **letters** in the English alphabet.
**2** Peter's uncle lives in America. Peter writes a **letter** to him every week.

# lettuce

*a green vegetable*
Anne likes eating **lettuce** in salads. She buys **lettuces** from the market.

# library

*plural* **libraries**
*a place where you can read books*
We have a new **library** in our school.

# lid

Alice is taking the **lid** off the box.

# lie

*verb* **lying, lay, lain**

**1** Peter is **lying** on the grass.
**2 to lie down**
Susan **lay down** and went to sleep.

*verb* **lying, lied, lied**
**3** *to say something that is not true*
That boy is twelve years old. "How old are you?" asked the man. "I'm fourteen," he said. He **lied** to the man.
*noun*
**4** *something that is not true*
That boy is twelve years old, but he told the man that he was fourteen. He told a **lie** to the man.

# life

**1** There are no plants or animals on the moon. There is no **life** on the moon.
**2** *plural* **lives**
Helen's grandfather had a very long **life**. He lived for eighty-seven years.

# lift

The box is very heavy. Tom cannot **lift** it.

# light

*noun*
**1** There are two **lights** in this room.

**2** The sun gives us **light**.
*adjective*
**3** *not heavy*
Lisa's bag is **light**. There is only one book in it.
**4** *not dark*
"What colour is Robert's car?" – "It is **light** blue."
*verb* **lighting, lit, lit**
**5** *to make something burn*
Steven **lit** a match, and then he **lit** the fire.

# lightning

There is some **lightning** in the sky.

# like

**1** *verb* **liking, liked, liked**
I **like** my friends. I love my brother and sister.
"Do you **like** apples, Tom?" – "Yes, I do. I eat a lot of apples."
**2** "What's string, mother?" – "String is **like** rope, but it is thinner."
Kate and her sister look **like** their mother.
**3** **would like**
"**Would** you **like** some tea?" – "No, thank you."
"I **would like** three kilos of oranges, please," Anne said to the greengrocer.

# likely

**likelier, likeliest**
*that you think will happen*
"Is Uncle Steven **likely** to come tonight?" – "Yes, he said he would try to come, so I think it's **likely**."

# lime

*a green fruit*
There are a lot of **limes** on our tree.

# line

**1** There are **lines** on the pages of this book.
**2** We catch fish with a fishing **line**.

# lion

*a large yellow animal*
**Lions** eat meat. They live in Africa.

# lip

*a part of the face*
We move our **lips** when we speak.

# liquid

Water, milk, and petrol are **liquids**. We can pour them.

# list

Anne is writing a **list** of the things she needs to buy.

# listen

Robert **listens** to the radio every morning.
"Tom, are you **listening** to me?" the teacher said. "Yes, I am." – "What did I say?"

# lit

*past and part of* **light**
My grandfather **lit** the fire.

# literature

*important books and stories*
Alan studies English **literature** at school. He likes the books of Charles Dickens best.

# litre

*a measurement of liquid*
There are two **litres** (2 **l**) of water in the bottle.

# little

**1** *not big*
There is a **little** bird in the tree.
**2 less, least**
*not much*
Paul has only got a **little** money. He has only got a few pounds.

# live

**living, lived, lived**
**1** "Where do you **live**?" – "I **live** in Italy."
**2** Helen's grandfather **lived** for eighty-seven years. He died in 1985.

# lives

*plural of* **life**
Tom likes reading about the **lives** of famous writers.

# living room

*a room in a house*
We watch television in the **living room** of our house.
**Sitting room** and **lounge** are other words for **living room**.

# loaf

*plural* **loaves**

Kate bought a **loaf** of bread at the baker's yesterday.

# lock

*to close with a key*
"Please **lock** the door when you leave, Peter. Here is the key."

# lonely

**lonelier, loneliest**
*without friends*
I am very **lonely**. My family is not here, and I have no friends in this town.

# long

**1** *not short*
The river is **long**. The tree is tall.

A hundred years is a **long** time.
**2** *a measurement of length*
"How **long** is that car?" – "It's four metres **long**."
**3** *a measurement of time*
"How **long** have you worked in that factory?" – "Two years."

# look

**1** When we want to know the time, we **look** at a clock.
**2** That house **looks** very small, but it has a lot of rooms.
"What does Martin **look like**?" – "He is tall and thin, and he has got a moustache."
**3 to look for**
Peter cannot find his pen. He is **looking for** it.
**4 to look out**
*to be careful*
"You must **look out** when you walk across a road!" Jane said to her children.
**5 to look after**
"Maria, I'm going to the shops. Please **look after** your little brother."

**6 to look forward to**
The students are **looking forward to** their holiday next week.

# lorry

*plural* **lorries**

Robert is driving a **lorry**.

# lose

**losing, lost, lost**
**1** "I can't find my watch. I think I have **lost** it."
**2** *not to win*
Tom and Nick had a race. Tom **lost** the race.
**3 to get lost**
Alan **got lost** in the big town. He couldn't find the station.

# lot or lots

**A lot of** children are playing in the school playground.
There are **lots of** children in the playground.

# loud

The bell is making a **loud** noise.

# lounge

*a room*
**1** We watch television in the **lounge** of our house.
**Sitting room** and **living room** are other words for **lounge**.
**2** We waited for the plane in the airport **lounge**.

# love

**loving, loved, loved**
**1** I **love** my mother and father. I like my teacher.
**2** *to like something very much*
Alan **loves** ice cream.

# lovely

**lovelier, loveliest**
*beautiful*
There are some **lovely** flowers in the garden.

# low

*not high*
**1** The plane is flying **low**. It is coming to the airport.

**2** There is a **low** wall in front of the house.

# luck

"Goodbye, Robert. I'm going to London tomorrow for my new job." – "Goodbye, Andrew, and **good luck**!" – "Thank you."

# luckily

We were late for the train, but **luckily** the train was late, too.

# lucky

**luckier, luckiest**
Jane is very **lucky**. She lost her ring in the street, but the next day she found it again.

# luggage

*the bags and other things that you take with you when you travel*
When Christopher went to America, he took a lot of **luggage**.

# lunch

We have **lunch** in the middle of the day. We have dinner in the evening.

# lying

**1** *part of the verb* **lie, lay, lain**
"Where's that cat?" – "It is **lying** under the table."
**2** *part of the verb* **lie, lied, lied**
That boy says that he is fourteen years old, but I think that he is younger. I think that he is **lying**.

# Mm

# machine

Cars and televisions are **machines**.
There are a lot of **machines** in factories.
Elaine has got a **sewing machine** for making clothes.

# made

*past and part of* **make**
Jane **made** lunch for us.
Keys are **made of** metal.

# magazine

*a short book with pictures that you buy each week or month*
Alan likes reading **magazines** about cars.

# magic

*strange things which happen that you cannot understand*
At the theatre we saw a man take a lot of things out of a very small box. We couldn't understand how he did it. It was **magic**!

# make

**making, made, made**

**1** Louise is **making** a cake.

Babies **make** a lot of noise when they cry.
This television was **made** in Japan.

**2** The teacher **made** the students do their work very quietly.

The smell of food **makes** me feel hungry.

**3 to make money**
*to earn*
That man **makes** a lot of **money** every week, because he has a good job.

**4 to make up**
*to think of something new*
The students **made up** a story. Then they wrote it in their books.

## male

Steven is a man. He is **male**. Jane is a woman. She is female.

## man

*plural* **men**
Steven is a **man**. Jane is a woman.

## manager

*the most important person in a shop or factory*
Martin is the **manager** of a bottle factory.

## mango

*plural* **mangoes**
*a yellow fruit*
**Mangoes** grow on trees. They are sweet.

## many

**1 more, most**
*a lot of*
There are **many** different kinds of birds.
There are not **many** trees in the desert, because there isn't much water.

**2 how many**
"**How many** oranges did you buy?" – "I bought six."

## map

Jenny is looking at a **map** of Europe.

## march

**marches, marching, marched, marched**

The soldiers are **marching**.

## March

*the third month of the year*
There are thirty-one days in **March**.

## mark

*noun*
**1** My little brother has put some **marks** on the wall.

**2** The teacher gave Susan a good **mark** for her English work, because everything was right.

**3 question mark**
This is a **question mark**    ?

We write a **question mark** after a question, like this: "How old are you?"

**4 exclamation mark**
This is an **exclamation mark**    !
We sometimes use an **exclamation mark** when we write things that people say: "Helen, come here!"

*verb*
**5** *to write on something and show if it is right or wrong*
We wrote some sentences in English. Our teacher **marked** them.

## market

Alice is buying some fruit in the **market**.

## marriage

George and Mary got married in 1944. Mary died in 1984. Their **marriage** lasted forty years.

## married

*verb*
**1** *past and part of* **marry**
Janet **married** David in 1975. They **got married** on July the tenth.
*adjective*
**2** Janet is **married to** David. She is his wife. He is her husband.

## marry

**marries, marrying, married, married**
Isabel is **marrying** Martin today. A lot of people are coming to the wedding.
Janet **married** David in 1975.

# marvellous

*very good*
"Do you like Charles Dickens' books?" – "Yes, I think they're **marvellous**."

# match

*plural* **matches**

**1** There is a box of **matches** on the table.

**2** The boys watched the football **match** between England and Spain.

# material

Metal, paper and glass are **materials**. We make things from them.

# mathematics or maths

In the **mathematics** lesson we learn about numbers.
Peter is good at **maths**.

# matter

*verb*
**1** *to be important*
"I am late for the bus." – "It doesn't **matter**. There will be another bus in five minutes."
*noun*
**2** "**What's the matter?**"
"Lisa, why are you crying? **What's the matter?**" – "I can't find my camera."

# maximum

*biggest*
The **maximum** temperature yesterday was thirty degrees centigrade (30°C).

# may

**1** "I don't know when your grandfather will come. He **may** come tonight or he **may** come tomorrow."
**2** "I feel ill. Please **may** I leave the room?" said Peter. "Yes, of course you **may**," his teacher said.

# May

*the fifth month of the year*
There are thirty-one days in **May**.

# maybe

"Will Uncle David come tomorrow?" – "I don't know. **Maybe** – but **maybe** he is still in London."
**Perhaps** is another word for **maybe**.

# me

"I need a pen. Can you give **me** your pen for a minute, please?"
I went to the cafe. Nick came with **me**.

# meal

Breakfast, lunch and dinner are **meals**.

# mean

**meaning, meant, meant**
**1** "What does 'foreign' **mean**?" – "It **means** 'not from this country'."
**2** "Did you bring your camera?" – "No, I'm sorry. I **meant** to bring it, but I forgot."

# meaning

"Do you know the **meaning** of the word 'foreign'?" – "No, I don't." – "It means 'not from this country'."

# measure

**measuring, measured, measured**
Jenny is **measuring** her plant. It is twenty centimetres tall.

# measurement

"What are the **measurements** of this room?" – "It's five metres long, four metres wide, and three metres high."

# meat

We buy **meat** from the butcher. The **meat** of a sheep is called "lamb".

# mechanic

Robert is a **mechanic**. He knows a lot about cars.

# medicine

*things that the doctor gives us when we are ill*
Tom had some green **medicine** when he was ill.

# medium

*not big or small*
Sam is tall. Andrew is short. James is of **medium** height.

Sam    James    Andrew

# meet

**meeting, met, met**
1 "Are we going to the cinema tonight?" – "Yes. **Meet** me at the cinema at seven o'clock."
2 "Do you know Lisa's brother?" – "No, I've never **met** him."
3 **"Pleased to meet you."**
"Peter, this is my friend Julie" – **"Pleased to meet you**, Julie."

# meeting

Every month, all the teachers have a **meeting**. At the **meeting** they talk about their students' work.

# melon

*a round fruit*
We can buy **melons** in the market.

# member

*a person who is in a group*
Peter is a **member** of the school football team.

# memory

*plural* **memories**
Tom has a good **memory**. He remembers everything that he reads or learns.

# men

*plural of* **man**
There are two **men** in my house: my father and my uncle.

# mend

There was no picture on our television. My father **mended** it. Now we can watch it again.

# menu

*a list of the food that you can eat in a cafe or restaurant*
Tom read the **menu**. Then he told the waiter what he wanted to eat.

# message

"Please give this **message** to your brother. Tell him that I want to see him tomorrow."

# met

*past and part of* **meet**
I **met** Isobel in the market this morning.

# metal

Gold and iron are **metals**.
Keys are made of **metal**.

# metre

*a measurement of length*
One **metre** equals one hundred centimetres (1**m** = 100cm).
Paul is one and a half **metres** tall.

# mice

*plural of* **mouse**
The **mice** ate the cheese.

# microphone

*something that makes things louder*
This man is speaking into a **microphone**.

# midday

*twelve o'clock in the middle of the day*
At **midday** the sun is very hot.

# middle

There are some flowers in the **middle** of the table.

We have lunch in the **middle** of the day.

# midnight

*twelve o'clock at night*
I go to bed at **midnight**.

# might

"Have you got any ten pence coins?" – "I **might** have some. I'll look in my purse."

# mile

*a measurement of length*
One **mile** is a little more than 1600 metres.
"How far is it to the sea?" – "It's about three **miles**."

# milk

We get **milk** from cows and goats.
Lisa drinks a glass of **milk** every morning.

# millimetre

*a measurement of length*
A thousand millimetres equal one metre (1000**mm** = 1m).
Some insects are only one or two **millimetres** long.

# million

*the number* **1,000,000**
More than eight **million** people live in London.

# mind

**1** "Do you want tea or coffee?"
– "I don't **mind**. I like tea and coffee."
**2 "Would you mind…?"**
**"Would you mind** carrying this box for me, Peter?" – "Of course I will, mother."
**3 "Never mind."**
"I'm sorry, but I can't come to the cinema with you tonight."
– "**Never mind.** We can go to the cinema tomorrow."

# mine

**1** "That is my book." – "No, it's **mine**. Look, here's my name in the front."
**2** *a big hole under the ground where people dig out coal or metals or jewels*
Andrew works in a **mine**.

# miner

*a man who works in a mine*
Andrew is a **miner**. He works under the ground.

# minimum

*smallest*
The **minimum** temperature yesterday was four degrees centigrade (4°C).

# minus

Six **minus** two equals four
(6 − 2 = 4). Six plus two equals eight (6 + 2 = 8).

# minute

**1** *a part of an hour*
There are sixty **minutes** in an hour.
**2 for a minute**
*for a short time*
"Can I look at your newspaper **for a minute**, please?" – "Of course."

# mirror

Nick is looking at his face in the **mirror**.

# miss

**misses, missing, missed, missed**
**1** *not to get the bus, train, or plane that you want*
"Why are you late?"–
"Because I **missed** the bus."
**2** *not to catch something*
Peter threw the orange to his sister. She **missed** it. The orange fell on the floor.
**3** *to be sad because you are not with someone*
My brother is studying in London. I **miss** him a lot.

# Miss

Susan's teacher is not married. She is called **Miss** Jameson.

# missing

David's children are **missing**. Everyone is looking for them, but no one can find them.

# mistake

"You made a **mistake**. You said that Paris was in Spain. That's not right! Paris is in France."

# mix

**mixes, mixing, mixed, mixed**
*to put together*
We **mix** flour, eggs, butter, and sugar to make a cake.

# mixture

*things that are put together*
"What are you eating?" – "I'm eating a **mixture** of meat, rice, and vegetables."

# model

These boys are playing with **model** aeroplanes.

# modern

*new*
Jane's kitchen is very **modern**. She has a lot of machines in it to help her.

# moment

We went into the classroom for the first lesson at nine o'clock. At that **moment** the bell rang.

# Monday

Today is **Monday**. Yesterday was Sunday. Tomorrow will be Tuesday.
On **Mondays** we have an English lesson at school.

# money

"Have you got any **money**?" – "Yes, I've got one pound and forty pence."
A car costs a lot of **money**.

# monkey

*an animal*
These are **monkeys**.

# month

*a part of a year*
There are twelve **months** in a year.
January is the first **month** of the year.

# moon

It is night. The **moon** is in the sky.

# more

1 Cars cost **more** than bicycles.
2 Cars are **more** expensive than bicycles.
3 There are twenty students, but we only have fifteen books. We need **more** books.
4 "Is there **any more** coffee?" – "Yes." – "Can I have **some more**, please?"
5 There are **no more** apples. We must buy some today.
6 **not … any more**
When Steven was young he lived in Bristol, but now he lives in London. He does **not** live in Bristol **any more**.

# morning

1 We have breakfast in the **morning.**
2 "**Good morning.**"
"**Good morning**, Robert" – "**Good morning**, George. How are you today?" – "Very well, thank you."

# most

1 **Most** children like ice cream.
**Most** cars have four doors.
"Have we got any oranges?" – "We've eaten **most of** them, but there are a few in that bowl."

2 I study French, English, and German. They are all difficult, but German is the **most** difficult.

# moth

*an insect with four wings*
**Moths** fly at night.

# mother

Paul is helping his **mother** in the kitchen.

# motorbike or motorcycle

*a big bicycle with an engine*
Martin goes to work on his **motorbike** every day.

# motorway

*an important road between big towns*
There are a lot of cars and lorries on the **motorway** to London.

# mountain

There are a lot of **mountains** in Europe.

# mouse

*plural* **mice**

*a small animal with a long tail*
This is a **mouse**.

# moustache

Steven has a **moustache**.

moustache

# mouth

mouth
*a part of the face*
This is Kate's **mouth**.

# move

**moving, moved, moved**

1 The car is **moving**. The lorry is not **moving**.
2 Helen **moved** her chair to the front of the classroom.

# movie

*a film*
We are going to the cinema tomorrow. We are going to see a **movie**.

# Mr

Simon Smith is called "**Mr** Smith" at his office. His friends call him "Simon".

# Mrs

Diane is Simon Smith's wife. Most people call her "**Mrs** Smith". Her friends call her "Diane".

# much

**1 more, most**
*a lot of*
There isn't **much** water in the bottle.

There is not **much** grass in the desert, and there are not many trees.
**2** An elephant is **much** stronger than a horse.
**3 how much**
"**How much** sugar do you want?" – "A kilo, please."
**4 how much**
"**How much** is this pen?" – "It's two pounds."
**5 very much**
"Here's a present for you." – "Thank you **very much**."

# mud

*wet earth*
The farmer is walking in the **mud** beside the river. His feet are very dirty.

# multiply

**multiplies, multiplying, multiplied, multiplied**
Two **multiplied** by three is six (2 x 3 = 6).

# mum or mummy

*a name that children call their mother*
"Can we go to the shops, **mummy**?" said the little boy. "Yes, we can," said his mother.

# museum

*a building with many old things in it*
You can see very old swords in the British **Museum**.

# music

"Do you like listening to **music**?" – "Yes. I like Elvis Presley and The Beatles."

# musician

When Elvis Presley sang, some **musicians** played the music for him.

# must

**1** We **must** have water and food to live.
When you drive a car, you **must** stop when a policeman tells you to stop.
**2** "That man has a big house and two cars. I think he **must** have a lot of money."

# mustn't

*must not*
"You **mustn't** make a noise, because the baby is sleeping."

# my

"Is that **my** pen?" – "No, that is Tom's pen. Here is your pen."

# myself

**1** I cut **myself** when I opened a tin this morning.
**2** *without any help*
"Did your mother make that dress?" – "No, I made it **myself**."
**3 by myself**
*without any other person*
I walk to school **by myself** every day.

# Nn

# nail

nail

nail

**1** We have a **nail** on each finger.
**2** Martin made a table. He used some **nails**.

# name

"What's your **name**?" – "My **name** is Alan."

# narrow

This street is very **narrow**.

# nasty

**nastier, nastiest**
*not nice*
Flies are **nasty**. I don't like them.

# national

*of a country*
Robert plays football for England. He plays for the English **national** football team.

# nationality

*plural* **nationalities**
"What **nationality** are you?" – "I am Spanish."

# naughty

**naughtier, naughtiest**
When a child does something bad, we say he is **naughty**.
"You have broken your toy, you **naughty** boy!" said the little boy's mother.

# near

There is a tree **near** the house.

# nearly

"What's the time?" – "It's **nearly** three o'clock."

# necessary

Today is a school holiday. It is not **necessary** to get up early.

# neck

neck

*a part of the body*
Your **neck** is between your head and your shoulders.

# necklace

Maria's sister is wearing a **necklace**.

necklace

# need

**1** Plants **need** water. They cannot live without water.
**2** We **need** to buy some sugar today. We haven't got any sugar.

# needle

needle

Kate is using a **needle**.

# needn't

*need not*
We **needn't** get up early today. Today is a holiday.

# neighbour

**1** Louise is talking to her **neighbour**.

**2** France and Spain are **neighbours**. France is next to Spain.

# neither

**1** Tom and Peter cannot buy an ice cream. **Neither** of them has any money.
**2 neither** … **nor**
Helen doesn't like rice, and her sister doesn't like rice. **Neither** Helen **nor** her sister likes rice.

# nephew

*the son of your brother or your sister*
My sister has a child called Alan. Alan is my **nephew**.

# nest

The bird is sitting in the **nest**.

nest

# net

There is a big fish in the **net**.

# netball

*a game for two teams that you play with a ball*
The girls are playing **netball**.

# never

**1** It **never** snows in the desert.
"Have you ever been to America?" – "No, I've **never** been there."

67

**2 "Never mind."**
"I'm sorry, I can't come to the cinema with you tonight." – "**Never mind.** We can go to the cinema tomorrow."

# new

Tom's bicycle is very old. He wants a **new** bicycle.

# news

A newspaper gives us the **news**. It tells us all the things that are happening in our country and in other countries.

# newspaper

David is reading a **newspaper**.

# next

**1** *coming after*
"First I went to the market, and **next** I went to the baker's." – "What did you do **next**?" – "I came home."
The school holidays will start **next** week.
I didn't see the Rockie Mountains when I went to America. **Next time** I go there, I will go and see them.

**2 next to**
*beside*
Jenny is sitting **next to** her grandmother.

**3 next door**
My friend lives in the house beside my house. She lives **next door**.

# nice

**nicer, nicest**
Lisa lives in a very **nice** house. It is new, and it has a lot of rooms.
We like our new teacher. She's very **nice**.

# niece

*the daughter of your brother or your sister*
My brother has a child called Helen. Helen is my **niece**.

# night

The **night** comes after the day. You can see the moon **at night**.

# nine

*the number* **9**
There are **nine** people in my family.
Six plus three equals **nine** (6 + 3 = **9**).

# nineteen

*the number* **19**
My sister is **nineteen** years old.
Ten plus nine equals **nineteen** (10 + 9 = **19**).

# ninety

*the number* **90**
My grandmother is **ninety** years old.
Forty plus fifty equals **ninety** (40 + 50 = **90**).
This pen costs **ninety**-five (95) pence.

# ninth

September is the **ninth** month of the year.
Martin's birthday is on March the **ninth** (March **9th**).

# no

**1** "Is Paris in Spain?" – "**No,** it isn't. It's in France."
**2** There are **no** students in the school today. Today is a holiday.

# nobody

**Nobody** is in the classroom. Everyone is outside in the playground.
**No one** is another way of saying **nobody**.

# noise

The bell is making a lot of **noise**.

# noisy

**noisier, noisiest**
The lorries on this road are very **noisy**. They make a lot of noise.

# none

*not any*
Today is a holiday. **None** of the students is at school today.
The man in the market had some oranges, but he sold them all. Now he has **none**.

# nonsense

*something which does not mean anything*
"Eggs grow on trees." –
"That's **nonsense**!"

# noon

*twelve o'clock in the middle of the day*
At **noon** the sun is very hot.

# no one

**No one** is in the classroom. All the students are in the playground.
**Nobody** is another word for **no one**.

# nor

**1** Nick did not watch television last night. **Nor** did his brother. They went to the cinema.
**2 Neither … nor**
Helen doesn't like rice, and her sister doesn't like rice. **Neither** Helen **nor** her sister likes rice.

# north

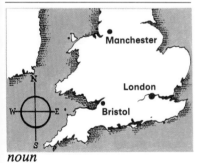

*noun*
**1** Manchester is in the **north** of England.
*adjective*
**2** New York is in **North** America.
Manchester is **north of** Bristol.

# northern

Manchester is in **northern** England.
Paris is in the **northern** part of France.

# nose

*a part of the face*
This is Kate's **nose**.

# not

**1** We go to school on Mondays. We do **not** go to school on Sundays.
**2** "Why **not**?"
"Peter isn't coming with us tonight." – "**Why not?**" –
"He's got a lot of work to do."

# note

**1** Mark must do a lot of things today. He wrote a **note** of all the things he must do.

**2** *a piece of paper money*
This is an English five pound **note**.

# nothing

There is **nothing** in the box.

# notice

*verb* **noticing, noticed, noticed**
**1** *to see*
"Lisa is wearing a new dress. Did you **notice** it?"

**2 to take notice**
Maria asked her father a question, but he did not **take** any **notice**. He was reading his newspaper.

*noun*
**3** Nick is looking at the **notice**. It says that there will be a school holiday tomorrow.

# nought

*the number* **0**
The number 100 has two **noughts**.

# noun

*a word for a person, a thing, or a place*
"Boy", "table", and "London" are **nouns**.

# November

*the eleventh month of the year*
There are thirty days in **November**.

# now

"Where's Uncle Steven?" –
"He's at work **now**. He will be here at four o'clock."

# nowhere

*in no place*
Peter cannot find his pen. He has looked in every part of the room. The pen is **nowhere** in the room.

# number

1, 2, 3, 4, 5 are **numbers**.
A, B, C, D, E are letters.

# nurse

Jane is a **nurse**. She works in a hospital.

# nut

These are **nuts**.

# nylon

*noun*
**1** *a cloth that clothes are made from*
Tom's shirt is made of **nylon**.
*adjective*
**2** Tom is wearing a **nylon** shirt.

# O o

# obey

*to do what someone tells you to do*
"Stop talking!" said the teacher. Everyone **obeyed** him. After that there was no more noise in the classroom.

# object

*a thing*
"What's that red **object** in the sky?" – "I think it's a kite."

# ocean

*a very big sea*
The Indian **Ocean** is between Africa and India.

# o'clock

"What's the time?" – "It's two **o'clock** (2.00)."

# October

*the tenth month of the year*
There are thirty-one days in **October**.

# of

**1** "What's the name **of** that student?" – "His name is Tom."
**2** One **of** my brothers is a butcher.
**3** "A kilo **of** sugar and a packet **of** tea, please."
**4** Robert's shirt is made **of** cotton.

# off

**1** *away from*
The cat is jumping **off** the wall.

**2** *not on*
The light in the classroom is **off**.
**3** *not at work*
The grocer does not work on Sundays. He has the day **off**.

# offer

Kate **offered** us some coffee. "Would you like some coffee?" she said.

# office

Isabel works in an **office**. She is a secretary.

# often

*many times*
I **often** go to the cinema.
"**How often** do you go to the shops?" – "I go every day."

# Oh!

**1** "Where is my pen?" said Lisa. "I can't find it. **Oh!** Here it is!"
**2** "**Oh dear!**"
The little boy fell down and cut his leg. "**Oh dear!**" his sister said.

# oil

**1** *a black liquid that gives heat when it burns*
We get **oil** from the ground. We can make petrol from **oil**.

**2** We cook food with **cooking oil**.

# OK

*yes*
"Do you want to go to the cinema with us, Kate?" – "**OK**."

# old

**1** *not young*
My grandmother is very **old**. She was born in 1912.
**2** *not new*
Tom's bicycle is very **old**. He wants a new bicycle.
**3** "How **old** is Nick?" – "He is fourteen years **old**."

# olive

*a small fruit*
**Olives** are black or green.

# on

**1** The book is
**on** the table.

The post office is **on** the left of the street.
**2** Peter went to the hospital **on** Monday.
**3** "It's dark in here. Put the light **on**."
**4** "What's **on** television this evening?" – "There is some football."

# once

**1** Kate goes to the shops **once** a week. She goes every Wednesday.
**2** *a long time ago*
**Once** there were fields here, but now there are big houses and offices.
**Once upon a time** there was a king who had a beautiful daughter…
**3 at once**
*now*
"Go to bed **at once**, Paul. It's very late."

# one

**1** *the number* 1
There is only **one** train to London today.
**One** plus **one** equals two
(1 + 1 = 2).

**2** There were two boys there. **One** of them was fat, but the other **one** was thin.

**3** Peter and Lisa have got cameras. The big **one** is Peter's, and the small **one** is Lisa's.
**4 one another**
Nick, Tom, and Peter are talking to **one another**.

# onion

*a vegetable*
We can buy **onions** in the market.

# only

**1** *no more than*
There is **only** one person in the street.

This bread is hot. The baker made it **only** ten minutes ago.
**2** Lisa is the **only** girl in our class who can swim.

# open

*verb*
**1** Peter **opened** the door and walked out of the room.
*adjective*
**2** "The door is **open**. Please close it."

# opposite

**1** The school is **opposite** the shops.
**2** The shops are here. The school is on the **opposite** side of the street.
**3** "Good" is the **opposite** of "bad". "Light" is the **opposite** of "dark".

# or

**1** "Are you going to the shops today **or** tomorrow?" – "Today."
**2 either … or**
"Do you want a drink? You can have **either** tea **or** coffee." – "Tea, please."

# orange

*noun*
**1** *a round fruit*
These are **oranges**.
**2** *a colour*
**Orange** is my favourite colour.
*adjective*
**3** Maria's dress is **orange**.

# order

*noun*
**1** These numbers are in **order**: 1 2 3 4. These numbers are not in **order**: 3 1 2 4.
**2** Peter went into a cafe. The waiter said to him: "Can I have your **order**, please?" – "Some coffee, please."
*verb*
**3** Peter **ordered** some coffee in the cafe.

# ordinary

*not different or special*
Today was an **ordinary** day. I got up, went to school, came home, did some work, and then went to bed.

# other

**1** I have two brothers. One works in an office. My **other** brother is a student.
Some of the students are in the classroom. The **others** are in the playground.
**2 each other**
Peter and Tom are friends. They like **each other**.

# ought

*should*
We **ought** to help our family, and we **ought** to do good things for other people.

# our

We have a car. **Our** car is red.

# ours

Your house is new, but **ours** is old.

# ourselves

**1** We like playing football. We enjoy **ourselves** when we play football.
**2** *without any help*
"Who made this table?" – "We made it **ourselves**."
**3 by ourselves**
*without any other person*
We walk to school **by ourselves** every day.

# out

**1** Tom opened the door and walked **out**.

Some people are coming **out of** the shop.
**2** Lisa is not at home. She is **out**.
**3** *not burning*
The fire is **out**. We must light it again.

# outdoors

*not in a building*
Martin doesn't work in a building. He is a farmer. He works **outdoors**.

# outside

**1** Susan is talking to her sister. Her sister is standing **outside** the house.
**2** Nick put on his coat and went **outside**.
**3** The **outside** of a watermelon is green. The inside is red.

# oven

The baker is putting some bread in the **oven**.

# over

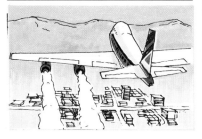

**1** You can see a plane flying **over** the town.
**2** *on top of*
Anne put on a coat **over** her dress.
**3** *more than*
"How much did it cost?" – "I don't remember, but it cost **over** five pounds."
**4** *finished*
School is **over**. Now everyone is going home.
**5 over there**
"Where's Tom?" – "He's **over there**, near the door."

# owe

**owing, owed, owed**
Last week my brother gave me fifty pence. Now I **owe** him fifty pence. I will give the money to him next week.

# own

**1** "Is that your **own** bicycle?" – "No, it isn't. It's my brother's."
Helen and Lisa have a room together, but I have a room **of my own**.
**2 on your own**
*without other people*
Kate likes to talk to other people, but Maria likes to be **on her own**.
**3** *to have something*
I **own** a bicycle. My father **owns** a car.

# Pp

## pack

*to put things in a bag or box*
Christopher is **packing** his clothes. Tomorrow he is going to America.

## packet

Martin is opening a **packet** of tea.

## page

There are a hundred and twenty-eight **pages** in this book.

## paid

*past and part of* **pay**
After the meal, Tom **paid** the waiter.

## pain

Helen has a broken arm. It gives here a lot of **pain**. She cannot sleep very well because of the **pain**.

## paint

*verb*
**1** Martin is **painting** the walls of his house.

*noun*
**2** Martin is putting some white **paint** on the walls of his house.

## painting

*a picture that you make with paint*
Michael is doing a **painting** of some boats.

## pair

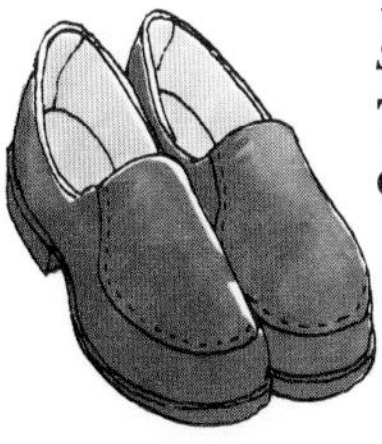

**1** *two of something*
This is a **pair** of shoes.

**2** Nick bought a new **pair** of trousers.
Susan cut the paper with a **pair** of scissors.

## palace

*a building where a king or an important person lives*
The Queen of England lives in Buckingham **Palace**.

## palm

**1** *a tree*
**Palm** trees grow in hot countries.

**2** *a part of your hand*
Peter has some coins in the **palm** of his hand.

## paper

**1** We write on **paper**.
Helen wrote her friend's address on a **piece of paper**.
**2** A **paper** is another word for a newspaper.

## parachute

The woman is falling through the air on a **parachute**.

## paragraph

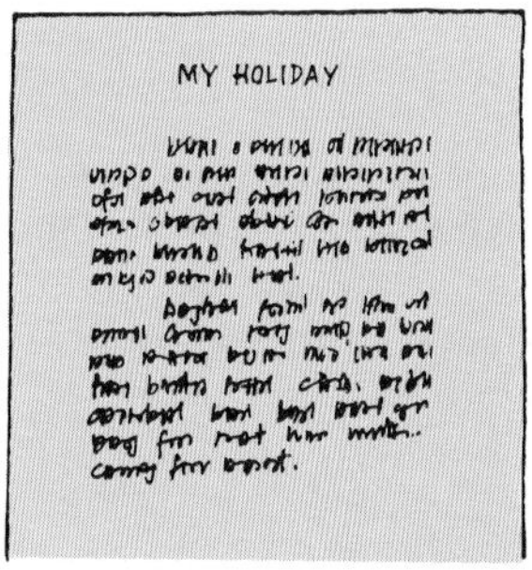


Maria wrote two **paragraphs** about her holiday in the lesson yesterday.

# parcel

Jenny is tying some string round a **parcel**.

# pardon?

"What's the time, Nick?" – "**Pardon**?" – "What's the time?" – "Oh, it's five past ten."

# parents

*your father and mother*
Steven and Jane are Peter's **parents**.

# park

*noun*
**1** Some people are walking in the **park**.
**2 car park**
*a place where you leave a car, bus, or lorry*
Robert left his car in a **car park** when he went to the cinema.
*verb*
**3** *to leave a car, bus, or lorry somewhere*
"Where did you **park** the car?" – "I **parked** in front of that block of flats."
**4 No Parking**
You must not park where there is a **No Parking** sign.

# parrot

*a bird*
We saw a red and green **parrot** in the zoo today.

# part

**1** *some of a thing, not all of it*
Tom, Alan, and Michael each had **part** of the cake.
We only go to school for **part** of the day.
**2** In this dictionary you will see:
  **swum**
  *part of* **swim**
This means that "swum" comes from the verb "swim".
**3 to take part**
*to do something with other people*
Nick **took part** in our game of football. He played very well.

# partly

*not all*
The Pyrenees mountains are **partly** in France and **partly** in Spain.

# party

*plural* **parties**
Today is my birthday. Our family is having a **party**. There are lots of nice things to eat and drink.

# pass

**passes, passing, passed, passed**

**1** The car is **passing** the bus.
**2** *not to fail*
Kate was very happy when she **passed** her English exam.

# passage

**1** *a narrow path in a building*
Helen walked along the **passage** to the classroom.
**2** *a short piece of writing*
The teacher gave us a **passage** about England to read.

# passenger

There are a lot of **passengers** on the bus.

# passport

You must show your **passport** when you go to a foreign country.

# past

**1** "Where is the station?" – "Go **past** the hospital and **past** the shops, and you will see it."
**2** "What's the time?" – "It's twenty **past** ten (10.20)."
**3** *many years ago*
In **the past**, people did not have electricity or gas.

**4** "Played" is the **past** tense of the verb "play". "Plays" and "is playing" are present tenses. In this dictionary you will see:

**went**

*past of* **go**

This means that "went" is the **past** tense of the verb "go".

# path

*a narrow road*
We went down the **path** to the river.

# pay

**paying, paid, paid**
*to give money for something*
"How much did you **pay** for that pen?" – "I **paid** fifty pence."
We had some ice cream in a cafe, and then we **paid** the waiter.

# P.E.

*a school subject*
The boys are having a **P.E.** lesson.
**P.E.** is a short way of writing **physical education**.

# pea

*a small green vegetable*
Robert is going to cook some **peas**.

# peace

*a time when there is no war or fighting*
Everybody wants **peace** in the world.

# peach

*plural* **peaches**
*a yellow and red fruit*
Anne bought some **peaches** at the market.

# peanut

Children like eating **peanuts**.

# pear

*a yellow and green fruit*
Susan likes **pears**.

# pen

Lisa writes with a **pen**.

# pence

*the name of the coins in England*
There are a hundred **pence** in one pound (100**p** = £1).
I've got a ten **pence** coin and a fifty **pence** coin.

# pencil

We can write and draw with a **pencil**.

# pen friend

*a friend in another country to whom you write letters*
Helen has a **pen friend** in Spain. Her **pen friend** is called Carmen.

# penguin

*a large bird*
**Penguins** live in cold countries. They cannot fly, but they can swim under water.

# people

*plural of* **person**
There are a lot of **people** in the shop today.

# pepper

**1** *a red or green vegetable*
You can buy **peppers** in the market.

**2** *something that we make from the seeds of a plant*
We sometimes put salt and **pepper** on our food when we eat it.

# per

**1** *for each*
This car can go at a hundred and sixty kilometres **per** hour.
**2** *per cent*
*of each hundred*
Eighty out of the two hundred students at our school are boys. Forty **per cent** (40%) of the students are boys.

# perfect

*with nothing wrong*
Alan's work was **perfect**. All his answers were right.

# perfectly

Alan answered the questions **perfectly**. He did not make any mistakes.

# perhaps

"Are you going to see Robert today?" – "I don't know. **Perhaps**." – "If you see him, please give him this."

**Maybe** is another word for **perhaps**.

# period

**1** *a length of time*
In the summer, there is a long **period** without rain in some countries.
**2** *a lesson*
The first **period** at school is from nine o'clock to ten o'clock.

# person

*plural* **people**

*a man, woman, or child*
There is only one **person** in the street.

# pet

*an animal that you keep in your house*
Jenny has two **pets** – a cat and a dog.

# petrol

**1** The man is putting some **petrol** in Robert's car.

**2 petrol station**
Robert is buying some petrol at the **petrol station**.
**Garage** is another word for **petrol station**.

# phone

*noun*
**1** *a telephone*
"Can I use your **phone**, please?" – "Of course."
*verb* **phoning, phoned, phoned**
**2** *to speak to someone using a telephone*
Lisa **phoned** her friend in London.

# photo or photograph

Lisa used her new camera this morning. She took some **photos** of her brother.

# photographer

*a person who takes photographs*
"What's your job?" – "I'm a **photographer**. I take photos of people and sell them."

# physical education

*a school subject*
We have **physical education** on Tuesdays. Sometimes we play football, and sometimes we do exercises.
**P.E.** is a short way of writing **physical education**.

# physics

Nick studies **physics** at school. This week he learnt about light and electricity. **Physics** is his favourite subject.

# piano

Jenny is playing the **piano**.

# pick

**1** *to take with your fingers*
Peter **picked** some apples from the tree.
**2** *to choose*
The teacher **picked** some boys for the football team.
**3** *to pick up*
*to take something into your hand*
Tom dropped the books. He **picked** them **up**.
**4** *to pick up*
*to go to get someone or something*
Robert went to the station and **picked** his aunt **up** in his car.

# picnic

*a time of eating outside*
The children are going to have a **picnic** near the river tomorrow.

# picture

There is a **picture** of our father on the wall.

# piece

*a part of something*
"Have you got a **piece** of paper? I want to write a letter."
Lisa had a **piece** of her mother's cake for lunch.

# pig

*an animal*
These **pigs** are on a farm.

# pill

*a medicine*
When Susan was ill, the doctor gave her some **pills**.

# pillow

Alice is putting a **pillow** on her bed.

# pilot

*a person who flies a plane*
William is a **pilot**. He works for British Airways.

# pin

Maria is making a dress. She is using some **pins**.

# pineapple

*a large fruit*
We can buy **pineapples** in the market.

# ping-pong

*a game for two people that you play with a small ball on a table*
Maria and Susan are playing **ping-pong**.
**Table tennis** is another way of saying **ping-pong**.

# pink

*a colour*
*noun*
**1** We make **pink** when we put red and white together.
*adjective*
**2** Lisa has got a **pink** dress.

# pipe

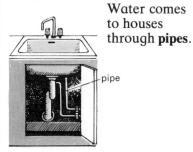

Water comes to houses through **pipes**.

pipe

# place

**1** Lions live in hot **places**. Penguins live in cold **places**.
**2 place of birth**
"What is your **place of birth**?" – "I was born in London."

# plan

*noun*
**1** This is a **plan** of the school buildings.
**2** "What are your **plans** for your holiday?" – "I want to see some friends in London, and I want to go to France, too."
*verb* **planning, planned, planned**
**3** *to think about what you are going to do in the future*
I **plan** to see my uncle when I go to London.

# plane

There is a **plane** in the sky.
**Aeroplane** is another word for **plane**.

# planet

The Earth is a **planet**. The **planets** go round the sun.

# plant

*noun*
**1** This is a **plant**.
Vegetables, flowers, and trees are **plants**.

*verb*
**2** *to put something in the ground to grow*
David **planted** a tree outside his house last year.

# plastic

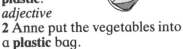

*noun*
**1** This bottle is made of **plastic**.
*adjective*
**2** Anne put the vegetables into a **plastic** bag.

# plate

plate

Michael is putting some food on his **plate**. He is taking it from the dish.

# play

*verb*
**1** My little sister is **playing** with her friends.
**2** Nick **played** football this morning.
**3** William is a musician. He **plays** the piano.
*noun*
**4** *a story that you see in a theatre*
We saw a very good **play** at the theatre yesterday.

# player

There are eleven **players** in a football team.

# playground

The children are in the school **playground**.

# please

"Can I have a piece of cake, **please**?" – "Yes, here you are." – "Thank you."
"**Please** carry this box for me." – "Yes, of course."

# pleased

**1** *happy*
Nick has a new bicycle. He is very **pleased**.
**2** "**Pleased to meet you.**"
"Helen, this is my friend Elaine." – "**Pleased to meet you**, Elaine."

# plenty

*a lot*
Babies need **plenty** of milk.

# plough

*noun*
**1** *something that you use when you turn over the earth in a field*
The farmer is using a **plough**.
*verb*
**2** *to turn over the earth in a field*
The farmer **ploughs** his fields every year.

# plural

*more than one*
The **plural** of "bag" is "bags".
The **plural** of "man" is "men".
In this dictionary you will see:
   **man**
   *plural* **men**

# plus

*and*
Seven **plus** three equals ten ($7 + 3 = 10$). Seven minus three equals four ($7 - 3 = 4$).

# p.m.

*in the afternoon or evening*
The bus leaves at seven **p.m.** (7.00 **p.m.**)

# pocket

Nick's hands are in his **pockets**.

# pocket money

*money that a mother and father give to their children every week*
Kate gets some **pocket money** every week.

# poem

Shakespeare wrote many famous **poems** as well as his plays.
**Poems** often rhyme.

# poetry

*poems*
We listened to some **poetry** in the class today.

# point

*verb*
**1** The teacher is **pointing** to the blackboard.
*noun*
**2** We write with the **point** of a pencil.
**3** We say "2.5" or "2,5" like this: "Two **point** five".
**4** At the end of the game, Nick had nine **points**, and I had ten **points**. I won the game.
**5** *the most important idea*
"What's the **point** of going to school, mother?" – "You go to school to learn things, Paul."

# poison

*something that can kill you if you eat it or drink it*
Some plants have **poison** in them. We must not eat them.

# police

**1** The **police** are trying to find a thief. He took some money from Andrew's shop.
**2 police station**
*the place where policemen work*
Someone took Robert's car today. Robert went to the **police station** and told the police.

# policeman

*plural* **policemen**

The **policeman** is stopping the cars.

# polish

*verb* **polishes, polishing, polished, polished**
**1** *to clean something until it shines*
Steven **polishes** his shoes before he goes to work.
*noun*
**2** *something that you use to make things shine*
Jane put some **polish** on the table.

# polite

**politer, politest**
Nick is very **polite**. He always says "please" and "thank you".

# pool

**1** *a lot of water on the ground*
After the rain, there were **pools** of water on the road.

**2** *a place where you can swim that is not the sea or a river*
Christopher likes swimming in the swimming **pool** at his hotel.

# poor

*not having much money*
That man is very **poor**, because he hasn't got a job.

# popular

*liked by many people*
Football is a very **popular** game. People play football in most countries of the world.

# population

*the number of people who live in a place*
Britain has a **population** of more than fifty-eight million.

# pork

*the meat of a pig*
We had **pork** and vegetables for dinner.

# possible

*that can be or can happen*
It is **possible** to go from London to Bristol by train, by bus, or by car.

# post

*verb*
**1** Susan is **posting** a letter to her brother.

*noun*
**2** We send letters by **post**.

# postbox

*plural* **postboxes**
*a box where you can post letters*
Susan put the letter in the **postbox**.

# postcard

*a card that you write on and send by post*

David wrote a **postcard** to his mother and father when he was on holiday in America.

# postman

*plural* **postmen**
*a person who brings letters to your home or your office*
The **postman** delivered three letters today.

# post office

At the **post office**, we post letters and buy stamps.

# pot

1 Alice is putting some vegetables in a **pot**.

2 *something that we use for keeping things in*
There is a **pot** of jam on the table.

# potato

*plural* **potatoes**
*a vegetable*
Anne bought some **potatoes** in the market.

# pound

1 *a measurement of weight*
One kilogram equals 2.2 **pounds** (1kg = 2.2**lb**).
Louise bought two **pounds** of onions in the market.
2 *the name of the money of some countries*
There are a hundred pence in one English **pound** (100p = £1).

# pour

Maria is **pouring** some water from the jug.

# powerful

*very strong*
Michael is a **powerful** swimmer, because his arms and legs are very strong.

# practice

*doing something many times*
William is a good swimmer because he has had a lot of **practice**.

# practise

**practising, practised, practised**
*to do something many times*
If you want to be a good swimmer, you must **practise** every day.

# prefer

**preferring, preferred, preferred**
*to like one thing more than another thing*
Helen likes tea, but she **prefers** coffee.

# prepare

**preparing, prepared, prepared**

Mark is **preparing** the dinner. The family are going to eat in half an hour.

# preposition

"Into", "at", and "with" are **prepositions**.

# present

*noun*
1 Lisa got some nice **presents** for her birthday. Her mother gave her a bicycle, and Susan gave her a kite.
*adjective*
2 "Walks" and "is walking" are **present** tenses of the verb "walk". "Walked" is the past tense.
3 *here*
Yesterday Nick did not come to school, but today he is **present**.

# press

**presses, pressing, pressed, pressed**

*to push down on something*
Helen is **pressing** the bell.

# pretend

It was very late at night, but Paul was reading his book in bed. When his mother came in he **pretended** to be asleep.

# pretty

**prettier, prettiest**
*nice to look at*
Kate's new dress is very **pretty**.
Helen's little sister is **pretty**.

# price

*the money that you must pay for something*
"What is the **price** of this pen?" – "Forty pence."

# primary

*first*
Children go to **primary** school when they are five years old.

# prince

*the son of a king or a queen*

# princess

*plural* **princesses**
*the daughter of a king or a queen, or the wife of a prince*

# prison

*a place where people must go when they do very bad things*
That man took some money from a shop. Now he is in **prison**.

# prize

*something that you get if you win, or if you are very good at something*
Susan's French is very good. She won the school **prize** for French.

# probable

*that you think will happen*
There are a lot of clouds in the sky. It is **probable** that it will rain.

# probably

There are a lot of clouds in the sky. It will **probably** rain today.

# problem

**1** *a question that you must find the answer for*
In the lesson, the teacher gave us some **problems**.
**2** *a difficult thing that you must do something about*
"I'm sorry we're late. We had a **problem** with our car."

# programme

Last night we watched a **programme** about France on television.

# promise

**promising, promised, promised**
*to say that you will do something*
"You **promised** to come and see me yesterday, but you didn't come. Why not?"

# properly

Those children cannot swim **properly**. They try, but they do not know how to swim.

# proud

*feeling pleased about something you have got or something you have done*
Nick is very **proud** of his new bicycle.

# public

*for everyone*
A park is a **public** place.

# pudding

*a sweet food that you eat at the end of a meal*
We had lamb for dinner yesterday, and then we had ice cream for **pudding**.

# pull

This little girl is **pulling** her toy.

# pump

*verb*
**1** *to move liquids or air with a machine*
The men are **pumping** water from the river.

*noun*
**2** The **pump** is taking water from the river.

**3 bicycle pump**
Peter put some air into the tyres of his bicycle with a **bicycle pump**.

# pupil

Tom is a **pupil** at a school in London. His brother is a student at London University.

# puppet

The children are watching the **puppets**.

# purple

*a colour*
*noun*
**1** We make **purple** when we put red and blue together.
*adjective*
**2** Susan sometimes wears a **purple** dress.

# purse

Jane keeps her money in a **purse**.

# push

**pushes, pushing, pushed, pushed**

Robert is **pushing** his car.

## put

**putting, put, put**

**1** Lisa is **putting** a plate on the table.

**2 to put away**
*to put in a cupboard*
After playing with their toys, the children **put** them **away**.

**3 to put on**
Michael is **putting on** his shoes. He wears them at school. When he comes home, he **puts** his slippers **on**.

## pyjamas

Paul is going to bed. He is wearing **pyjamas**.

## pyramid

Many people go to see the **pyramids** in Egypt.

# Q q

## quantity

*plural* **quantities**
*an amount*
Jane buys potatoes in large **quantities**, because everyone in her family eats a lot of potatoes.

## quarrel

*verb* **quarrelling, quarrelled, quarrelled**
**1** *to talk in an angry way with someone*
Peter and his sister **quarrelled** about what to watch on television.
*noun*
**2** Peter and his sister had a **quarrel** about what to watch on television.

## quarter

**1** Thirty out of forty boys in our class can swim. Three **quarters** ($\frac{3}{4}$) of the class can swim.
**2** "What's the time?" – "It's a **quarter** to six."

## queen

**1** *a woman who is the ruler of a country*
**Queen** Elizabeth is the **Queen** of England.
**2** *the wife of the king of a country*

## question

**1** "How many days are there in a year?" – "That's a difficult **question**. 350 days?" – "No, the answer is 365 days."
**2 question mark**
This is a **question mark**       ?
We write a **question mark** after a question, like this: "What is your name**?**"

## queue

*a line of people*
There is a long **queue** of people at the bus stop. They are waiting for the bus.

## quick

*not slow*
Lisa was late for school. She had a **quick** breakfast, and then she ran to school.

## quickly

*not slowly*
Lisa ate her breakfast **quickly** because she was late for school.

## quiet

*without noise*
At night, our house is very **quiet**.
"**Be quiet!**" the teacher said to the students. "Stop talking!"

## quietly

The students were making no noise. They were reading their books **quietly**.

## quite

Our village is small. Bristol is **quite** big. London is very big.

## quiz

*plural* **quizzes**
**1** We had a **quiz** at school today. The teacher asked us a lot of questions about animals. The student who answered most questions won the **quiz**.
**2 quiz show**
We watched a **quiz show** on television yesterday. A lady got all the answers right. She won a new car.

# R r

## rabbit

*a small animal*
There are some **rabbits** in the field.

## race

The boys had a **race**. They all ran very fast. Nick was the fastest: he won the **race**.

## racket

We play tennis with a tennis **racket**.

## radar

*a machine that shows you where things that you cannot see are*
Many ships and planes have **radar**.

## radio

George listens to the news on the **radio** every morning.

## rail

**1** *a long piece of metal*
Trains go on two **rails**.
**2 by rail**
*on a train*
Martin went from Paris to Madrid **by rail**.

## railway

**1** "Is there a **railway** from London to Bristol" – "Yes, you can take a train from London to Bristol."
**2 railway station**
*a place where trains stop*
Robert is going to the **railway station**. He is going to get a train to London.

## rain

*noun*
**1** *water that comes from the sky*
There was a lot of **rain** yesterday. The roads were very wet.
I went for walk **in the rain**.
*verb*
**2** There are dark clouds in the sky. It is going to **rain**.

## raincoat

It is raining. Christopher is wearing a **raincoat**.

## rainy

**rainier, rainiest**
*with a lot of rain*
Last week was very **rainy**. It rained every day.

## raise

**raising, raised, raised**

*to lift up*
The students **raise** their hands when they know the answer to the teacher's question.

## ran

*past of* **run**
Nick **ran** to school yesterday because he was late.

## rang

*past of* **ring**
The teacher **rang** the school bell and the students went into the classroom.

## rat

*a small animal*
**Rats** have long tails.

## rather

**1** *a little*
"It's a nice day today." – "Yes, but it's **rather** cold."
**2** "Would you like to go swimming or would you **rather** play tennis?" – "It's cold today, so I'd **rather** play tennis."

# reach

**reaches, reaching, reached, reached**

**1** *to be able to get something with your hand*
Peter is trying to get the apple, but he cannot **reach** it.
**2** *to get to a place*
The train left London at three o'clock and **reached** Bristol at six o'clock.

# read

**reading, read, read**
Robert **reads** the newspaper every morning.

# ready

We can eat now. Dinner is **ready**.
"Are you **ready** to go?" – "No, but I'll be **ready** in five minutes."

# real

"Is that a **real** diamond?" – "No! It's made of glass."

# really

"Are those boys **really** fighting?" – "No, they are only playing."

# reason

*why something happens or why someone does something*
"What's the **reason** for your visit to Paris?" – "I want to see my uncle."

# receive

**receiving, received, received**
*to get something from someone*
Maria **received** a letter from her aunt today.

# recognize

**recognizing, recognized, recognized**
*to know someone or something again*
I did not see my uncle for many years, but I **recognized** him when I saw him at the airport.

# record

**1** Mark is listening to a **record** of Mozart music.
**2** **record player**
The record is on the **record player**.

# rectangle

A **rectangle** has two long sides and two shorter sides.

# red

*the colour of blood*
*noun*
**1 Red** is my favourite colour.
*adjective* **redder, reddest**
**2** The teacher writes on our books with a **red** pen.

# reflection

Nick can see a **reflection** of his face in the mirror.

# refrigerator

*a machine which makes food cold*
"Where's the milk?" – "It's in the **refrigerator**."
**Fridge** is a short way of saying **refrigerator**.

# refuse

**refusing, refused, refused**
*to say "no" to something*
Helen asked her brother to help her. He **refused**, because he was busy.

# regular

**1** *happening every day, week, or year at the same time*
There is a **regular** train from here to London. It leaves every day at ten o'clock.
**2** "Walk" (walking, walked, walked) is a **regular** verb. "See" (seeing, saw, seen) is an irregular verb.)

# relative

*a person in the same family*
George is a **relative** of Lisa's. He is her grandfather.

# remain

*to stay*
Peter went to the cinema, but his brother **remained** at home.

# remember

"When is the holiday?" – "I don't know. The teacher told me, but I can't **remember**."

# rent

*noun*
**1** *money that you pay for living*

in a building or for using a shop
The **rent** for this house is a
hundred pounds a month.
*verb*
**2** *to pay money so that you can
live or work in a building*
Martin **rents** a flat near the
station.

# repair

*verb*
**1** Robert is **repairing** his car.
*noun*
**2** This house is very old. It
needs a lot of **repairs**.

# repeat

*to say again*
"I didn't hear what you said.
Could you **repeat** it, please?"

# reply

*verb* **replies, replying, replied,
replied**
**1** *to answer*
"What's the time?" Maria
asked. "Six o'clock," Helen
**replied**.
*noun, plural* **replies**
**2** *an answer*
I wrote a letter to my aunt, but
I did not get a **reply** from her.

# report

*verb*
**1** *to speak or write about
something that has happened*
Robert drove his car into a
shop window. The next day the
newspaper **reported** the story.
*noun*
**2** *the story of something that has
happened*
There was a **report** about the
accident in the television news.

# reporter

*a person who writes in a
newspaper, or who speaks
about what has happened on
television or on the radio*
Sam is a **reporter**. He writes
about football for "The Daily
News".

# reptile

*an animal which has cold blood
and which comes from an egg*
Snakes are **reptiles**.

# rescue

**rescuing, rescued, rescued**
A little boy fell into the river.
He could not swim. Peter
jumped into the water and
**rescued** him.

# rest

**1** *a time with no work or play*
Every day, Anne has a **rest** for
an hour after lunch.
**2** *to have a time with no work or
play*
Anne **rests** for an hour every
afternoon.
**3 the rest of**
*all the other people or things*
Some of the students are in the
classroom. **The rest of** them are
in the playground.

# restaurant

A lot of people are eating in
this **restaurant**.

# result

*something that happens because
of another thing*
"What was the **result** of your
talk with David?" – "We
decided to go to America next
week."

# return

*verb*
**1** *to come back to a place*
David went to Bristol in the
morning. He **returned** to
London in the afternoon.
*noun*
**2** *a ticket to a place and back
again*
"A ticket to London, please."
– "A single or a **return**?" – "A
**return**, please."

# reward

*something that you give to a
person who has done something
good*
Steven has lost his bag. He will
give a **reward** of five pounds to
the person who finds it.

# rhyme

*noun*
**1** This is a **rhyme**:
   "One, two,
   Put on my shoe.
   Three, four,
   Open the door."
*verb* **rhyming, rhymed, rhymed**
**2** "Two" **rhymes** with "shoe".
"Four" **rhymes** with "door".

# rice

**Rice** grows in fields. It needs a
lot of water.
We sometimes eat **rice** for
dinner.

# rich

Douglas is very **rich**. He has a lot of money.

# ride

**riding, rode, ridden**

Peter is **riding** his bicyle.
Nick sometimes **rides** a horse.

# right

**1** "Two and two are five." – "No, that's wrong." – "Two and two are four." – "Yes, that's **right**!"
**2** Most people write with their **right** hand, not with their left hand.

**3** The school is on the **right** of the street. The school is on the **right-hand side** of the street. The shops are on the left.
**4** all right
"Was the film good?" – "No, but it was **all right**."
"Please hold this for me." – "**All right**. Give it to me."

# ring

*noun*
**1** Some people wear **rings** on their fingers.

*verb* **ringing, rang, rung**
**2** The teacher **rings** the bell at the end of the lesson.

**3** The lesson stops when the school bell **rings**.

# ripe

**riper, ripest**
*ready to be eaten*
You cannot eat those tomatoes now. They are not **ripe**.

# rise

*verb* **rising, rose, risen**
*to go up*
**1** The sun **rises** early in the morning.
**2** There was a lot of rain yesterday. The water in the river has **risen**.
*noun*
**3** *becoming higher*
There was a **rise** in the price of sugar last month.

# river

The Nile is a very long **river**.

# road

This is a **road** to London.

# roar

*to make an angry noise*
The lion saw the man and **roared**.

# rob

**robbing, robbed, robbed**
*to take something that is not yours from somebody*
Some men **robbed** Andrew. They took all his money.

# robbery

*plural* **robberies**
*taking money or things that are not yours*
There was a **robbery** at Andrew's shop. Some men took all Andrew's money.

# robot

This is a **robot**.

# rock

There are a lot of **rocks** in this part of the river.

# rocket

The **rocket** is leaving the Earth.

# rode

*past of* **ride**
Peter **rode** his bicycle to school yesterday.

# roll

The ball is **rolling** along the ground.

# roof

There is a bird on the **roof** of Alan's house.

# room

There are five **rooms** in our house: a kitchen, a bathroom, a sitting room, and two bedrooms.

# root

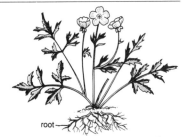

*the part of a plant that is under the ground*
Plants take water in through their **roots**.

# rope

This man has his horse on a **rope**.

# rose

*noun*
**1** *a beautiful flower*
There are a lot of **roses** in our garden.

*verb*
**2** *past of* **rise**
The water in the river **rose** after the rain last week.

# rough

**1** *not smooth*
This road is very **rough**.
**2** *moving a lot*
The sea was very **rough** yesterday because the wind was strong.

# round

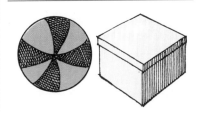

**1** This box is square. The ball is **round**.

**2** The moon goes **round** the Earth.

Our family sits **round** the table to have dinner.

# roundabout

The bus is going round the **roundabout**.

# row

*noun*
**1** *a line*
The children are standing in a **row,** waiting for the teacher.

*verb*
**2** *to make a boat move*
Michael is **rowing** the boat across the river.

# rub

**rubbing, rubbed, rubbed**
**1** *to move one thing backwards and forwards over another thing*
Kate **rubbed** her shoes with a cloth to make them clean.
**2 to rub out**
Tom writes in pencil. When he makes a mistake, he can **rub** the word **out** and write it again.

# rubber

**1** Tom writes in pencil. If he makes a mistake, he uses a **rubber**.
**2 Rubber** comes from trees. Some balls are made of **rubber**.

# rubbish

**1** *things that we do not want*
Maria is throwing some **rubbish** in the basket.

**2** "I ate two hundred eggs." – "That's **rubbish**! No one can do that!"

# rude

**ruder, rudest**
*not polite*
"Give me a cake," said the little boy. "You are very **rude**," said his mother. "You must say, 'Please can I have a cake?'."

# rule

*noun*
**1** *what someone says you must do or not do*
It is a school **rule** that we must not play with balls in the classroom.
*verb* **ruling, ruled ruled**
**2** *to be the king or the most important person in a country*
Napoleon **ruled** France for many years.
**3** *to draw a line with a ruler*
Maria **ruled** some lines in her book.

# ruler

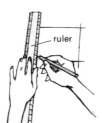

**1** Maria is drawing a line with her **ruler**.

**2** *the king or the most important person in a country*
Napoleon was a famous **ruler** of France.

# run

**running, ran, run**

The boys are **running** along the road. The girl is walking.

# rung

*part of* **ring**
"Let's go into the classroom. The bell has **rung** for the first lesson."

# runner

*a person who runs*
Nick is a good **runner**. His brother can run very well, too.

# rush

**rushes, rushing, rushed, rushed**
*to go fast*
Steven and Martin **rushed** to the station because they were late for their train.

# S s

# 's

**1** Nick**'s** book is blue. The green book is Tom**'s**.
**2** *is*
"Where**'s** Peter?" – "He**'s** outside."
**3** *has*
"Has Helen done her work?" – "Yes, she**'s** done all of it."

# sad

**sadder, saddest**
*not happy*
Helen is **sad** because her friend Maria is going to live in Madrid.

# safe

**safer, safest**
**1** This building is very old. It is not **safe**. You must not go in it. It might fall down.
**2** *not in danger*
The farmer shot the fox, and now his hens are **safe** again.

## safely

Martin drives very **safely**. He watches the road all the time, and he does not drive fast.

## said

*past and part of* **say**
I gave Helen some tea, and she **said**, "Thank you."

## sail

sail

*noun*
**1** This boat has white **sails**.
*verb*
**2** This boat is **sailing** on the sea.

## sailor

*a man who works on a ship at sea*
Sam is a **sailor**. He has been to many countries.

## salad

*vegetables which you eat cold*
Helen had a tomato and lettuce **salad** for lunch today.

## salesman

*plural* **salesmen**
"What's your job, Robert?" – "I'm a car **salesman**. I sell cars. People buy a lot of cars from me."

## salt

There is **salt** in the water in the sea.
Susan put some **salt** on her dinner.

## same

*not different*
These keys are the **same**.

These keys are different.

## sand

There is a lot of **sand** in the desert and on the beach.

## sandal

This is a pair of **sandals**.

## sandwich

*plural* **sandwiches**
Alan made a **sandwich**. He put some cheese between two pieces of bread.

## sang

*past of* **sing**
Elvis Presley **sang** very well. Everyone liked his songs.

## sank

*past of* **sink**
The boat **sank** in the storm.

## sat

*past and part of* **sit**
Yesterday I **sat** at the back of the class.

## Saturday

Today is **Saturday**. Yesterday was Friday. Tomorrow will be Sunday.

On **Saturdays** Peter plays football with his friends.

## saucepan

saucepan

Louise is cooking some food in a **saucepan**.

## saucer

There are two cups and **saucers** on the table.

saucer

## save

**saving, saved, saved**
**1** *to help someone to be safe*
Tom can't swim. When he fell into the river, I **saved** him. I pulled him out of the water.
**2** *to keep something for a future time*
Every month, my father gives me some money, and I **save** it. I don't spend it.

## saw

*verb*
**1** *past of* **see**
Kate **saw** a snake yesterday.

*noun*
**2** Martin is cutting some wood with a **saw**.

# say

**saying, said, said**
Peter **says** "Goodbye" to his mother when he leaves his house.
"Did you speak to Jane?" – "Yes. She **said** that Lisa is ill."

# scar

*a mark from an old cut*
I have a **scar** where I cut my arm last year.

# scarf

*plural* **scarves**
Helen is wearing a **scarf**.

In winter, Christopher wears a **scarf** around his neck.

# school

*a building where children study*
We go to **school** in the morning. We study a lot of things at **school**.
Maria's **school** is very big.

# science

In **science** lessons we learn about plants and animals, and about air, light, and water.

# scientist

*a person who studies science*
Some **scientists** study the plants and animals that live in the sea.

# scissors

Susan cut some paper with a pair of **scissors**.

"Have you got any **scissors**?" – "Yes, there are some here."

# score

*verb* **scoring, scored, scored**

**1** Peter is **scoring** a goal.
*noun*
**2** "What's the **score** in the football game?" – "The **score** is England 2, Spain 2."

# scratch

**scratches, scratching, scratched, scratched**

The cat has **scratched** Tom's arm.

# screw

*a small piece of metal that holds things together*
Martin is making a table. He is using **screws**.

# sea

The boys are swimming in the **sea**.

# season

*a part of the year*
There are four **seasons** in the year: spring, summer, autumn, and winter.

# seat

Our school bus has forty-five **seats**. Forty-five people can sit in the bus.

# seat belt

Robert is driving his car. He is wearing a **seat belt**.

seat belt

# second

*adjective*
**1** February is the **second** month of the year.
Today is June the **second** (June **2nd**).
*noun*
**2** *a part of a minute*
There are sixty **seconds** in a minute.

# secondary

My sister is eleven. This year she will go to **secondary** school. Last year she went to primary school.

# secret

*noun*
**1** *something that you do not tell other people*
"Where did you go on Monday?" – "I'm not going to tell you. It's a **secret**."
*adjective*
**2** A **secret** message is a letter that other people cannot read.

# secretary

*plural* **secretaries**

Isabel is a **secretary**. She works in an office.

# see

**seeing, saw, seen**
**1** Anne wears glasses because she cannot **see** very well.
"Did Paul write that letter?" – "Yes, I **saw** him doing it last night."
**2** *to visit*
Nick went to **see** his mother in hospital.
**3** *to understand*
"I don't **see** what you mean. Please explain again."

# seed

We put **seeds** in the earth. Plants and flowers grow from them.

# seem

Helen **seemed** sad. I asked her what was wrong. "Nothing's wrong," she said. "I'm not sad, I'm thinking."

# seen

*part of* **see**
"Have you **seen** Alan today?" – "Yes. I saw him this morning."

# sell

**selling, sold, sold**
A butcher **sells** meat. We buy meat from the butcher.

# send

**sending, sent, sent**
My brother **sent** me a present from America last week. Now I must **send** a letter to him to thank him.

# sentence

This is a **sentence**:
    I like oranges.
After a **sentence** we write . or ? or !

# September

*the ninth month of the year*
There are thirty days in **September**.

# serious

**1** *not laughing much*
Christopher is a very **serious** man. He does not laugh much, and he thinks a lot.
**2** *important*
"Mother, why isn't there enough food for everyone in the world?" – "That is a very **serious** question, Paul."

# set

**setting, set, set**
The sun **sets** in the evening. It goes down in the sky.

# seven

*the number* **7**
There are **seven** days in a week.

Ten minus three equals **seven** $(10 - 3 = 7)$.

# seventeen

*the number* **17**
Julie is **seventeen** years old.
Ten plus seven equals **seventeen** $(10 + 7 = 17)$.

# seventh

July is the **seventh** month of the year.
It is the **seventh** of November (**7th** November) today.

# seventy

*the number* **70**
There are **seventy** houses in my street.
Forty plus thirty equals **seventy** $(40 + 30 = 70)$.
My grandmother is **seventy**-two (**72**) years old.

# several

*more than two, but not many*
Michael has **several** friends in London.

# sew

**sewing, sewed, sewn**
Maria is **sewing**.

# sewing machine

*a machine which sews clothes*
Jenny is using a **sewing machine**.

# shade

*where it is dark because the light from the sun does not get there*
Alice and her friend are sitting in the **shade**. Mark is working in the sun.

# shadow

The sun is shining. You can see the **shadows** of the trees.

shadow

# shake

**shaking, shook, shaken**

**1** *to move something quickly up and down*
The nurse is **shaking** the bottle of medicine.

**2 to shake hands with**
Peter's father met the new teacher today. He **shook hands with** him.

# shall

"What **shall** we do tomorrow?" – "I don't know." – "**Shall** we go swimming?" – "Yes, let's go swimming in the river."

# shallow

*not deep*
This river is **shallow**. It is only one metre deep.

# shan't

*shall not*
"I **shan't** be at home tomorrow. I have to go to work."

# shape

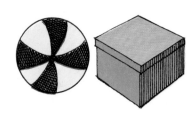

"What **shape** is a ball?" – "It's round."
"What **shape** is that box?" – "It's square."

# share

**sharing, shared, shared**
**1** *to have something with another person*
Helen **shares** a bedroom with her sister.
**2** *to give part of something to another person*
Michael **shared** the food with his friends.

# shark

*a large fish*
**Sharks** eat other fish.

# sharp

**1** *good to cut with*
I can't cut this meat because the knife isn't **sharp**.
**2** I can't write with this pencil because it isn't **sharp**.

# sharpen

*to make sharp*
**1** This knife is not sharp. I must **sharpen** it.

**2** Kate is **sharpening** her pencil.

# shave

**shaving, shaved, shaved**

David is **shaving**.

# shaver

Martin shaves with an **electric shaver**.

# she

Helen is my sister. **She** is fifteen years old.

## she'd

**1** *she would*
Helen said **she'd** be at home, but she was not there.
**2** *she had*
I went to see Susan, but **she'd** gone to the shops.

## sheep

*plural* **sheep**

*an animal*
There are some **sheep** in the field.

## sheet

**1** *a large piece of cloth that you put on a bed*
My mother puts clean **sheets** on my bed every week.
**2** *a flat piece of something that is thin*
Paul drew a picture on a **sheet** of paper.
Martin bought a **sheet** of glass for the window of his house.

## shelf

*plural* **shelves**
The bottle is on the **shelf**.

## she'll

*she will*
Maria is at school today, but **she'll** be at home tomorrow.

## shell

*the outside part of some animals, or of an egg, or of a nut*

We found a lot of **shells** near the sea yesterday.
The **shell** of an egg is very thin.

## shelves

*plural of* **shelf**
There are two **shelves** in our kitchen.

## she's

**1** *she is*
Kate is a student. **She's** a good student.
**2** *she has*
Jane has been to the market this morning. **She's** bought a lot of fruit.

## shine

**shining, shone, shone**
The sun is **shining**. It is very hot today.

## ship

This **ship** carries things across the sea.

## shirt

Alan is wearing a white **shirt**.

## shoe

This is a pair of **shoes**.

## shoemaker

Sam is a **shoemaker**. He makes very good shoes.

## shone

*past and part of* **shine**
The sun **shone** all day yesterday.

## shook

*past of* **shake**
Peter **shook** the box and the matches fell out.

## shoot

**shooting, shot, shot**

This soldier is **shooting** with his gun.

## shop

There are four **shops** in this street: a baker's, a toy shop, a grocer's and a greengrocer's.

## shop assistant

*someone who works in a shop*
The **shop assistant** in the grocer's sold me some coffee.

## shopkeeper

*someone who has a shop*
Andrew is a **shopkeeper**. He opens his shop at nine o'clock every morning.

## shopping

*buying things from shops or from the market*
Anne does most of her **shopping** in the market. She **goes shopping** every day.

## short

**1** *not long*
Alan's hair is **short**. His sister's hair is long.
**2** *not tall*
My young brother is very **short**. He cannot touch the top of the table.

## shorts

*short trousers*
Peter is wearing **shorts**.

— shorts

## shot

*past and part of* **shoot**
George **shot** a rabbit yesterday.

## should

"It's late. We **should** go home now, Tom." – "Yes, we **should**."

## shoulder

*a part of the body*
Tom is carrying a box on his **shoulder**.

## shouldn't

*should not*
Children **shouldn't** play in the street, because it's dangerous.

## shout

*verb*
**1** *to say something loudly*
Michael saw his friends a long way away. He **shouted** to them, but they could not hear him.
*noun*
**2** We heard a **shout** from the other side of the road. We looked across. It was our uncle.

## show

**showing, showed, shown**

Helen is **showing** her book to the teacher.
Tom **showed** us some photos of his holiday.

## shower

Mark is having a **shower**.

## shut

**shutting, shut, shut**

*to close*
Helen is **shutting** the door.

## sick

*ill*
Susan was **sick** yesterday. She didn't go to school. She was in bed all day.

## side

Nick is standing on one **side** of the classroom. Tom is sitting on the other **side**.
Nick has his hands **by his sides**.

## sight

Anne's **sight** is not very good. She cannot see very well.

# sights

*famous places that people go to see*

On our holiday in America, we saw many **sights**. We saw the White House, the Rockie Mountains, the Golden Gate Bridge, and the Mojave desert.

# sign

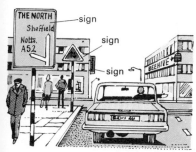

*noun*
**1** There are a lot of **signs** along this street.
*verb*
**2** *to write your name*
When you write a letter, you **sign** your name at the end.

# silence

The students did not talk. They worked in **silence**.

# silent

*not speaking*
"Why did you come home late, Paul?" his mother asked. Paul was **silent**. He did not answer.

# silk

*noun*
**1** *a cloth that clothes are made from*
**Silk** is an expensive material.
*adjective*
**2** Kate's mother has got a beautiful **silk** scarf.

# silly

**sillier, silliest**
The little boy was talking to his toy animal. "Don't be **silly**!" said his sister. "Toys can't talk."

# silver

*noun*
**1** *a metal*
Many old coins are made of **silver**.
*adjective*
**2** *the colour of this metal*
My grandfather's hair is **silver**.

# similar

Horses and donkeys are **similar** animals. Horses are **similar to** donkeys.

# simple

**simpler, simplest**
*not difficult*
The teacher's question was very **simple**. Everyone could answer it.

# since

**1** *from a time in the past to now*
George's brother has lived in Madrid **since** 1971. He has lived there for many years.
**2** *because*
Anne did not go outside, **since** it was very hot.

# sincerely

Sometimes Sam writes a letter to a person whom he does not know very well. Then he begins: "Dear Mr Smith", and he ends: "**Yours sincerely**, Sam Brown".

# sing

**singing, sang, sung**
Elvis Presley **sang** very well.

# singer

Elvis Presley was a very famous **singer**. He sang many songs.

# single

*noun*
**1** *a ticket to a place*
"Can I have a ticket to London, please?" – "A **single** or a return?" – "A **single**, please."
*adjective*
**2** *not married*
Helen is **single**, but her sister is married.

# singular

*one*
The **singular** of "baskets" is "basket".
The **singular** of "mice" is "mouse".

# sink

*noun*
**1** Paul is washing some plates in the **sink**.

*verb* **sinking, sank, sunk**
**2** *to go down in water*
The boat **sank** because there was a hole in it.

Metals **sink** in water. Wood floats on water.

# sister

Peter and Lisa have the same mother and father. Lisa is Peter's **sister**. Peter is Lisa's brother.

sit

## sit

sitting, sat, sat

**1** Lisa is **sitting** on a chair.

**2 to sit down**
We **sat down** and the teacher began the lesson.

## sitting room

*a room in a house*
Peter and Lisa are in the **sitting room**. They are watching television.
**Living room** and **lounge** are other words for **sitting room**.

## six

*the number* **6**
Robert goes to work **six** days a week.
Nine minus three equals **six** (9 − 3 = **6**)

## sixteen

*the number* **16**
Maria is **sixteen** years old.
Ten plus six equals **sixteen** (10 + 6 = **16**).

## sixth

June is the **sixth** month of the year.
Michael's birthday is on the **sixth** of April (**6th** April).

## sixty

*the number* **60**
My grandfather is **sixty** years old.
Twenty plus forty equals **sixty** (20 + 40 = **60**).
There are only **sixty**-seven (67) people in our village.

## size

"What **size** are those shoes?" – "**Size** 40." – "They're too small for me. I need **size** 42."

## skate

*verb*
skating, skated, skated
**1** Jenny is **skating** on the ice.
*noun*
**2** Jenny has **skates** on her feet.

## skeleton

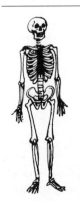

*all of a person's bones*
This is a **skeleton**.

## ski

*verb*
**1** Jenny is **skiing**.
*noun*
**2** Jenny has **skis** on her feet.

## skin

*the outside part of a person, or of an animal, or of a fruit*
We make shoes from the **skin** of animals.
The **skin** of a banana is yellow.

## skirt

Helen is wearing a **skirt**.

skirt

## sky

*plural* **skies**

At night you can see the moon in the **sky**.

## sleep

sleeping, slept, slept
**1** The baby is **sleeping**.

**2 to go to sleep**
Paul went to bed at ten o'clock.
He **went to sleep** ten minutes
later. He slept for eight hours.

# sleepy

**sleepier, sleepiest**
*wanting to sleep*
It was a very hot day, and after
lunch everyone was very
**sleepy**.

# slept

*past and part of* **sleep**
I **slept** well last night.

# slide

**sliding, slid, slid**

These children are **sliding** on
the ice.

# slip

**slipping, slipped, slipped**

*to begin to fall*
Alan **slipped**
because there
was some oil
on the road.

# slipper

Alice wears
**slippers** in the
evening.

# slow

*adjective*
**1** *not fast*
"Do you want to walk to the
cinema?" – "No, that's too
**slow**! We'll go by bus."
Robert went to London on a
**slow** train. It took an hour to
go forty kilometres.
*verb*
**2 to slow down**
The car **slowed down** and
stopped when the driver saw
the dog in the road.

# slowly

*not fast*
My grandfather is a very old
man. He walks very **slowly**.

# small

*not big*
Insects are very **small**.
Elephants are very big.
Paul goes to a **small** school. It
has only got forty-three
students.

# smell

*verb* **smelling, smelt** *or* **smelled,
smelt** *or* **smelled**
**1** You **smell** things with your
nose.
**2** Those flowers **smell** very nice.
*noun*
**3** There is a **smell** of fruit in the
market.

# smile

*verb* **smiling, smiled, smiled**

**1** *to show with
your face that
you are happy*
Helen is
**smiling**.

*noun*
**2** Helen has a **smile** on her
face.

# smoke

*noun*
**1** That fire is
making a lot
of **smoke**.

*verb* **smoking, smoked, smoked**
**2** That fire is **smoking** a lot.

# smooth

*not rough*
A baby has a very **smooth** skin.

# snack

*a small meal*
I sometimes eat a **snack**
between breakfast and lunch.

# snail

*a small animal*
This **snail** lives
in the garden.

# snake

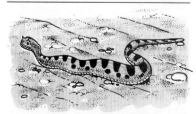

**Snakes** are long and thin. They
have no legs.

# snow

*noun*
**1 Snow** is white and soft. It falls from the sky when the weather is very cold.
*verb*
**2** It sometimes **snows** in England.

## so

**1** That box is **so** big that I can't carry it.
**2** Michael got up at half past nine, **so** he was late for school.
**3** Anne got up early **so** she could go to the shops.
Martin took a book **so that** he could read it on the train.
**4** "Are you coming to the cinema with us tonight?" – "I don't think **so**."
"Will you have a holiday this year?" – "I hope **so**."
**5** Peter's mother asked him to go to the market, and Peter did **so**.
**6** "I need a drink," said Tom. "**So** do I!" said Nick. "Let's go to the cafe."

## soap

Nick is washing his hands with some **soap**.

## social studies

*a school subject*
In the **social studies** lesson today we learned about how people live in other countries.

## sock

We wear **socks** on our feet.

## soft

**1** *not hard*
I like to sleep on a **soft** bed.
Bananas are a **soft** fruit.
**2** *not loud*
"The music is too **soft**. I can't hear it!"

## sold

*past and part of* **sell**
Peter has **sold** his kite to me.

## soldier

The **soldier** is standing in front of the gate.

## some

**1** "Have you got any money?" – "Yes. My brother gave me **some** this morning."
"Would you like **some** coffee?" – "Yes, please."
**2** *a part*
**Some** of the students are in the classroom, and the others are in the playground.

## somebody or someone

"I gave **somebody** my pen. Who did I give it to? Did I give it to **someone** in this class?"

## something

"I've got **something** for you." – "What is it?" – "It's a book."
"It's very hot today. I need **something** to drink."

## sometimes

**Sometimes** I go to school on my bicycle, and **sometimes** I go by bus.

## somewhere

"Where does Nick live?" – "He lives **somewhere** in London."

## son

This is Peter with his mother and father. He is their **son**.

## song

Elvis Presley was a singer. He sang a lot of good **songs**.

## soon

**1** *in a short time*
It is six o'clock in the evening. It will **soon** be dark.
**2** *as soon as*
"Here is the book. Please give it back to me **as soon as** you have read it."

## sore

Helen has cut her hand. Her hand is very **sore**.

## sorry

**1** "Peter, did you break this window?" – "Yes, father. I'm very **sorry**."
**2** "Do you want to come to the cinema?" – "I'm **sorry**, but I can't. I must do some work."
**3** *sad*
I am **sorry** to hear that Susan is ill.

## sort

"What is a parrot?" – "It's a **sort** of bird."
"What **sort** of fruit do you like?" – "I like oranges and bananas."

## sound

*noun*
1 "I can hear the **sound** of an aeroplane. Can you see it in the sky?"
*verb*
2 *to make a noise*
That bird **sounds** like a cat.
3 "Tomorrow we're going to the cinema and then to a cafe." – "That **sounds** nice!"

## soup

Maria had some vegetable **soup** for lunch yesterday.

## south

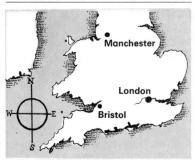

*noun*
1 Bristol is in the **south** of England.
*adjective*
2 Brazil is in **South** America.
Bristol is **south of** Manchester.

## southern

Bristol is in **southern** England. Granada is in the **southern** part of Spain.

## souvenir

*something that you buy because you want to remember a place*
David bought some **souvenirs** when he was on holiday in America.

## sow

**sowing, sowed, sown**
*to put seeds in the ground*
Last month the farmer **sowed** seeds in this field. Now you can see lots of small plants.

## space

Exercise 3

Yesterday I went to the market at 10 o'clock to buy so fruit fruit
I two
of

1 In this exercise, the students must write a word in each **space**.
2 *land with no buildings or trees on it*
"Let's play football near the river. There's a lot of **space** there."
3 Some men have flown through **space** to the moon.

## spaceship

This is a **spaceship**. It is going to the moon.

## speak

**speaking, spoke, spoken**
1 "I **spoke** to David this morning. He said that he will go to London tomorrow."
2 Christopher can **speak** Spanish and French very well.

## special

*different from most others*
Tomorrow is a **special** day. It is my birthday.

## speed

*how fast something moves*
"How fast is that car going?" – "Its **speed** is about ninety kilometres an hour."

## spell

**spelling, spelt *or* spelled, spelt *or* spelled**
I **spell** my name "Anne", but some people **spell** it "Ann".

## spelling

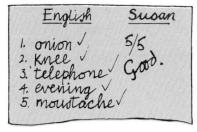

*the way you make a word from letters*
Susan is good at **spelling**.

## spend

**spending, spent, spent**
1 *to use money*
My mother **spends** about forty pounds every week. She **spends** it on food.
2 *to use time*
Maria **spent** two hours with her grandmother yesterday.

# spice

*a seed or a part of a plant that we put in food to make it taste better*
Isabel uses a lot of **spices** when she cooks.

# spider

*a small animal*
**Spiders** have eight legs. They eat insects.

# splash

*verb* **splashes, splashing, splashed, splashed**

**1** *to make someone or something wet*
Peter is **splashing** his friends with water.
*noun, plural* **splashes**
**2** There was a big **splash** when Tom fell into the water.

# spoke

*past of* **speak**
Peter's uncle is in London, but Peter **spoke** to him on the telephone yesterday.

# spoken

*part of* **speak**
"Have you **spoken** to the new student?" – "Yes, I spoke to her this morning."

# spoon

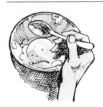

We eat ice cream with a **spoon**.

# spoonful

*what you can put in one spoon*
Susan is ill. Her mother must give her two **spoonfuls** of medicine every day.

# sport

"Which **sports** do you like?" – "I like football, tennis, and swimming."

# spot

Tom is ill. He has a lot of **spots** on his face.

# spread

**spreading, spread, spread**

**1** Jenny is **spreading** some jam on the bread.

**2** When you put oil on water, the oil **spreads** on top of the water.

# spring

*a part of the year*
**Spring** comes after winter and before summer.
In the **spring**, trees and plants begin to grow again.

# square

*noun*
**1** A **square** has four sides. The sides are all the same.
**2** There is a market in the **square** in the middle of our town.
*adjective*
**3** "What shape is this box?" – "It's **square**."

# stairs

Helen is walking down the **stairs**.

# stamp

Susan is putting a **stamp** on the letter.

# stand

**standing, stood, stood**

**1** Michael is **standing** next to the teacher. The teacher is sitting at his desk.

**2 to stand up**
We **stand up** when the teacher comes into the room.

# star

You can see lots of **stars** in the sky at night.

# start

The first lesson **starts** at nine o'clock and finishes at ten o'clock.
Helen **started** to learn French last year.

# station

**1** Trains leave from a **station**. Buses leave from a **bus station**.
**2 petrol station**
You can buy petrol at a **petrol station**.
**3 police station**
Policemen work in a **police station**.

# stay

**1** Yesterday I **stayed** at home. I didn't go out.
**2** *to be with someone for some time*
In the summer holidays, Maria **stays** with her aunt in Madrid.

# steal

**stealing, stole, stolen**
*to take something which is not yours*
Yesterday a thief **stole** some money from Susan's bag.

# steak

*a piece of meat*
Alice has bought a **steak** for her dinner.

# steam

*the gas that water becomes when it boils*
**Steam** is coming from the kettle.

# steel

*a strong metal*
Cars are made of **steel**.

# steep

It is difficult to walk up this hill. The hill is very **steep**.

# step

*noun*
**1** Jenny is walking up the **steps** to the school.

*verb* **stepping, stepped, stepped**
**2** *to put your foot down*
Peter **stepped** over the dog.

# stick

Christopher's grandfather is very old. He walks with a **stick**.

# still

**1** *to this time*
Susan started to learn French three years ago. She is **still** learning it now.
**2** *not moving*
"Sit **still**!" the teacher said to the students.

# stir

**stirring, stirred, stirred**
*to move something round with a spoon*
Isabel put some sugar in her coffee, and then she **stirred** it.

# stole

*past of* **steal**
A thief **stole** some money from Susan's bag in the shop yesterday.

# stolen

*part of* **steal**
"Someone has **stolen** my money!" shouted Susan.

# stomach

*a part of the body*
Michael ate too much for lunch today. Now his **stomach** hurts.

# stomachache

"I ate too much for lunch. Now my stomach hurts. I've got a **stomachache**."

# stone

There are a lot of **stones** in this field.

# stood

*past and part of* **stand**
We **stood** outside the classroom and waited for the teacher.

# stop

*verb* **stopping, stopped, stopped**
**1** The students **stopped** talking when the teacher came into the room.
**2** The bus **stopped** at the station and the people got out.
**3** The bus driver **stopped** his bus at the station.
*noun*
**4 full stop**
This is a **full stop**
We write a **full stop** at the end of a sentence.

# store

*verb* **storing, stored, stored**
**1** *to put something away for some time*
We **store** books in a big cupboard at the back of the classroom.
*noun*
**2** *a shop*
You can buy a lot of things at Andrew's **store**.

# stories

*plural of* **story**
Paul likes reading **stories** about children and animals.

# storm

*a time of bad weather, with a lot of wind and rain*
A tree fell down in the **storm** last night.

# story

*plural* **stories**
"What are you reading?" – "I'm reading a **story** about a king and his three sons."

# stove

Alice is cooking her dinner on the **stove**.

# straight

**1** This road is **straight**. The river is not **straight**.
**2** Tom walked **straight** home from school. He did not stop anywhere.

# strange

**stranger, strangest**
"That is a very **strange** noise. I don't know what it is."

# stranger

*someone whom you do not know*
"Who is that man?" – "I don't know. He's a **stranger** here."

# straw

The horse is lying on **straw**.

# strawberry

*plural* **strawberries**

*a small red fruit*
Susan likes **strawberries** very much.

"Can I have a **strawberry** ice cream, please?"

# street

*a road with buildings along it*
There are four shops in this **street**.

# string

There is some **string** round these books.

# stripe

*a long line on something*
Nick's shirt has **stripes** on it.

# striped

*with stripes*
Nick is wearing a **striped** shirt.

# strong

1 Christopher is a very **strong** man. He can carry heavy things.
2 The wind is very **strong** today.
3 Onions have a very **strong** smell.

# student

James is a **student**. He is studying at London University. His younger brother is a pupil at a school in London.

# study

**studies, studying, studied, studied**
*to learn about something in a classroom*
Susan **studies** the plays of Shakespeare at school.
Tom will **study** geography at university.

# stupid

That boy cannot swim, but he plays very near the river. He is very **stupid**.

# subject

"Which **subjects** do you like at school?" – "I like English, Spanish, and history."

# subtract

**Subtract** two from six, and you get four. (6 − 2 = 4).

# succeed

*to do something that you wanted to do very much*
Helen wanted to learn to swim. She tried for a long time. At last she **succeeded**.

# such

**1 such as**
You can buy a lot of food in the market, **such as** eggs, cheese, tomatoes, and oranges.
**2 such … that**
Robert has **such** a big car **that** eight people can get into it.

# suddenly

*quickly, when you do not think that something is going to happen*
A child ran in front of the bus. The bus stopped **suddenly**.

# sugar

*a sweet food*
Alan likes a lot of **sugar** in his coffee.

# suggest

*to give someone an idea*
"What shall we do this afternoon? Can you **suggest** anything?" – "I **suggest** that you go swimming." – "That's a good idea."

# suit

Christopher is wearing a **suit**.

# suitcase

*a large bag that you put clothes in*
This man is carrying two **suitcases**.
**Case** is a short way of saying **suitcase**.

# sum

These are **sums**.

# summer

*a part of the year*
**Summer** comes after spring. It is hotter than spring.
In the **summer** we have a school holiday.

# sun

The **sun** is shining in the sky.

# Sunday

Today is **Sunday**. Yesterday was Saturday. Tomorrow will be Monday.
On **Sundays** Tom goes to see his grandmother.

# sung

*part of* **sing**
"Have you **sung** this song before?" – "No, I haven't."

# sunk

*part of* **sink**
There are a lot of rocks in the sea near here. Many boats have hit them and **sunk**.

# sunny

**sunnier, sunniest**
Yesterday it was **sunny**. The sun shone all day.

# superlative

Most adjectives have a comparative and a **superlative**. The comparative of "high" is "higher". The **superlative** of "high" is "highest".
Mount Everest is *the highest* mountain in the world.

# supermarket

David went shopping in the **supermarket**. He bought everything that he needed there.

# supper

We had meat, potatoes, and vegetables for **supper**.
We have **supper** in the evening.

# sure

surer, surest
"What's the time?" – "It's only half past eight." – "Are you **sure**?" – "Yes. Look at my watch."

# surprise

*noun*
**1** *something that you did not know was going to happen*
Yesterday my father gave me a new football. It was a nice **surprise**.
*verb* **surprising, surprised, surprised**
**2** *to do something that someone did not think was going to happen*

My friend lives many kilometres away. He **surprised** me by coming to see me yesterday.

# swam

*past of* **swim**
Alan **swam** across the river yesterday.

# sweater

Tom is wearing a **sweater**.

sweater

# sweep

**sweeping, swept, swept**

Alice is **sweeping** the floor.

# sweet

*adjective*
**1** Sugar is **sweet**.
*noun*
**2** *a small thing with sugar in it that you eat*
Children like **sweets**.
**3** *something with sugar in it that you eat at the end of a meal*
We had meat and vegetables for dinner yesterday, and then we had a **sweet**. We had some ice cream.

# swept

*past and part of* **sweep**
Kate **swept** her bedroom.

# swim

**swimming, swam, swum**

The boys are **swimming** in the river.

# swimmer

Nick is a good **swimmer**. He can swim very well.

# swimming

Robert is good at **swimming**. He **goes swimming** every day.

# swimming pool

*a place for swimming that is not the sea or a river*
When we were on holiday, we swam in the hotel **swimming pool**.

# swing

**swinging, swung, swung**

*to move backwards and forwards through the air*
Jenny is **swinging** on a rope.

# switch

*noun, plural* **switches**

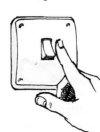

**1** "Turn the light on, please." – "Where's the **switch**?"

*verb* **switches, switching, switched, switched**
**2 to switch on**
"It's dark in this room. **Switch** the light **on**, please."
**3 to switch off**
Alan **switched** the television **off** and went to bed.

## sword

*a long knife for fighting*
This man is holding a **sword**.

## swum

*part of* **swim**
Nick can swim very well, but he has never **swum** across the river.

## swung

*past and part of* **swing**
"The door has **swung** open in the wind. Please close it."

# T t

## table

**1** There is some food on the **table**.

| STUDENTS | | | |
|---|---|---|---|
| YEAR | 1984 | 1985 | 1986 |
| BOYS | 194 | 181 | 170 |
| GIRLS | 203 | 196 | 184 |

**2** This is a **table**. It tells you the number of boys and girls in our school in 1984, 1985, and 1986.
There is a **table** of irregular verbs at the back of this dictionary.

## tablespoon

*a big spoon*
Michael put some rice on his plate with a **tablespoon**.

## table tennis

*a game for two people that you play with a small ball on a table*
Maria and Susan sometimes play **table tennis**.
**Ping-pong** is another way of saying **table tennis**.

## tail

A cat has a **tail**. Birds have **tails**, too.

tail
tail

## tailor

Martin is a **tailor**. He makes men's clothes and sells them.

## take

**taking, took, taken**

**taking, took, taken**
**1** Helen is giving her book to the teacher. The teacher is **taking** the book.
**2** *to carry or to go with*
My uncle **took** me to school in his car yesterday.
**3** *to need time*
"How long does it **take** to cook potatoes?" – "It **takes** about twenty minutes."
**4** *to take a photo*
Lisa **took a photo** of her family with her new camera.
**5** *to take off*
Peter put on his football clothes. He wore them to play football. Then he **took** them **off** and washed them.
**6** *to take off*
*to leave the ground*
The plane **took off** at six o'clock. It will land in Rome at nine o'clock.

## talk

*to speak*
Susan is **talking** to her friend. They are **talking about** their holidays.

# tall

**1** *not short*
The tree is **tall**.
The river is long.

**2** "How **tall** are you, Paul?" –
"I am one metre forty centimetres **tall**."

# tank

*something that holds a lot of liquid or gas*
There is a water **tank** in the roof of our house.
The petrol **tank** of my car is empty.

# tap

Nick is turning on the **tap**.

# taste

*noun*
**1** Sugar has a sweet **taste**.
*verb* **tasting, tasted, tasted**
**2** I like this food. It **tastes** very good.

# taught

*past and part of* **teach**
This week, our teacher has **taught** us how to write a letter in French.

# taxi

Martin drives a **taxi**. He takes people to a place in his car, and they pay him.

# tea

**1** Jenny is drinking a cup of **tea**.

**2** *a small meal in the afternoon*
In England, some people have **tea** at about five o'clock.

# teach

**teaches, teaching, taught, taught**
Last week, our teacher **taught** us about snakes. We learned about many different snakes.

# teacher

Nick's mother is a **teacher**. She teaches English.

# team

*people who play with others in a game*
There are eleven people in a football **team**.

# teapot

Isabel is putting some water in the **teapot**.

teapot

# tear 1

*noun*
**1** There is a **tear** in Nick's shirt.

*verb* **tearing, tore, torn**
**2** *to make a hole in*
Nick fell down from a tree and **tore** his shirt.

# tear 2

*water that comes from your eyes*
Lisa had **tears** in her eyes when she said goodbye to her family.

# teaspoon

*a small spoon*
Michael put sugar in his tea with a **teaspoon**.

# teeth

*plural of* **tooth**
We use our **teeth** when we eat.

# telephone

*noun*
**1** Lisa is using the **telephone**. She lives in London, but she is speaking to her friend in Paris.
*verb* **telephoning, telephoned, telephoned**
**2** *to speak to someone using a telephone*
Robert **telephoned** his brother in London.

**Phone** is another word for **telephone**.

# telescope

We look at the moon and the stars with a **telescope**.

# television

**1** We have a **television** in our house. It's a **colour television**.
**2** Peter and his sister like watching **television**.

"What's on **television** this evening?" – "There's some football."

**TV** is a short way of saying **television**.

# tell

**telling, told, told**
1 "Can you **tell** me the time, please?" – "Yes, it's ten o'clock."
Christopher **told** us **about** America. He **told** us **that** America is very big.
2 The teacher said, "Sit down." He **told** the students **to** sit down.

# temperature

Today it is very hot. The **temperature** is thirty-five degrees centigrade (35°C).

# temple

There are many old **temples** in Rome.

# ten

*the number* **10**
We have **ten** fingers and **ten** toes.
Six plus four equals **ten** (6 + 4 = **10**).

# tennis

*a game for two or four people that you play with a ball*
Mark and Jenny are playing **tennis**.

# tense

"Looks" and "is looking" are present **tenses** of the verb "look".
"Looked" is the past **tense** of the verb "look".
"Will look" and "is going to look" are future **tenses** of the verb "look".

# tent

These people are on holiday. They are living in a **tent**.

# tenth

October is the **tenth** month of the year.
David was born on May the **tenth** (May **10th**), 1948.

# term

*the time that you are at school between holidays*
This is the summer **term**. It ends in July.
In England, there are three **terms** in the school year.

# terrible

*very bad*
"I don't like this film. It's **terrible**!"

# test

*noun*
1 *a small exam*
The students must do a French **test** today. They must write the answers to the teacher's questions and give them to him.

*verb*
2 *to use something to see if it works*
Robert **tested** the car before he bought it.

# than

A horse is bigger **than** a donkey.
When you wash, it is better to use hot water **than** cold water.

# thank

*verb*
1 My brother bought me a new book. I **thanked** him.
2 "**Thank** you."
"This book is a present for you." – "**Thank you** very much!"
*noun*
3 "**Thanks!**"
"Here is your tea." – "**Thanks!**" said Robert.

# that

1 *plural* **those**

"This is my sister's book. **That** is my book."
2 I think **that** it will be cold tonight.
3 *which*
Helen is wearing the dress **that** her sister gave her.
4 "You go to my school, don't you?" – "Yes, **that's** right."

# the

1 There is a white cat in our garden. **The** cat is very small.
2 There are two bicycles outside our house. **The** new bicycle is Nick's. **The** old one is Michael's.

**3** Today is **the** sixth of July (6th July).
**4** Children like going to **the** cinema.
**5 The** sun is very hot.
Queen Elizabeth is **the** Queen of England.

# theatre

Kate is going to see a play at the **theatre** tonight.

# their

Peter and Paul are brothers. Lisa is **their** sister.

# theirs

"Look at Andrew and his brother in that big car. Is it their car?" – "No, it isn't **theirs**. It's Robert's car."

# them

"Did you see Kate and Maria?" – "Yes. I saw **them** at school."
"Where did you buy those bananas?" – "I bought **them** in the market."
"Did Tom's friends go to the zoo yesterday?" – "Yes. He went with **them**."

# themselves

**1** Lisa and Helen are watching television. They are enjoying **themselves**.
**2** *without any help*
Tom and Peter made this table **themselves**.
**3 by themselves**
*without any other person*
My young sisters must not go to the shops **by themselves**.

# then

**1** *at that time*
"Nick will be home at five o'clock. You can talk to him **then**."

**2** *after that*
Anne had breakfast. **Then** she went to the shops.

# there

**1** *in that place*
"Don't sit **there**! Come and sit here with me."
"I can't find my book ... Oh, **there** it is!"
**2 There** is a school near my house.
**There** are a hundred and twenty-eight pages in this book.

# therefore

*because of that*
Peter has hurt his leg.
**Therefore** he cannot play football today.

# there's

*there is*
**There's** a picture of our father on the wall.

# these

*plural of* **this**

"**These** pens cost fifteen pence. Those pens cost twenty-five pence."
"Are **these** your books?" – "Yes, they are. Thank you."

# they

"Where are Lisa and Susan?" – "**They** are at school."
"Have we got any oranges?" – "Yes, **they** are in that bowl."

# they'd

**1** *they would*
Nick and Peter said **they'd** be in the cafe, but they weren't.
**2** *they had*
"I went to see Lisa and Susan, but **they'd** gone to school."

# they'll

*they will*
My brother and sister are at school today, but **they'll** be at home tomorrow.

# they're

*they are*
"Where are Alan and Tom?" – "**They're** at school."

# they've

*they have*
Nick and Peter are happy. **They've** got new bicycles.

# thick

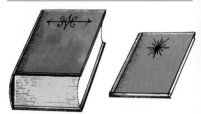

**1** *not thin*
The book on the left is **thick**. The book on the right is thin.
**2** "How **thick** is that wall?" – "It's twenty centimetres **thick**."

# thief

*plural* **thieves**
*a person who steals things*
In the shop yesterday a **thief** took some money from Susan's bag.

# thin

**thinner, thinnest**
**1** *not fat*
That woman is **thin**.

**2** *not thick*
This piece of paper is very **thin**.
I can see through it.

# thing

"What's this?" – "It's a **thing** for opening bottles."
I bought a lot of **things** in the market today – a shirt, three handkerchiefs, some coffee, and some vegetables.

# think

**thinking, thought, thought**
**1** The teacher asked a difficult question. The students **thought** for a time, and then they wrote the answer.
"What are you **thinking about**?" – "I'm **thinking about** my new bicycle."
**2** "What do you **think of** ...?"
"What do you **think of** my new dress?" – "I think it's very pretty."

# third

**1** March is the **third** month of the year.
My brother's birthday is on the **third** of May (**3rd** May).
**2** In our class there are twenty children who can swim and ten children who can't swim. Two **thirds** ($\frac{2}{3}$) of the class can swim. One **third** ($\frac{1}{3}$) of the class can't swim.

# thirsty

**thirstier, thirstiest**
The weather is very hot today. I am **thirsty**. I need a drink.

# thirteen

*the number* **13**
There are **thirteen** people on the bus.
Twenty minus seven equals **thirteen** ($20 - 7 = 13$).

# thirty

*the number* **30**
There are **thirty** days in April.
Twenty plus ten equals **thirty** ($20 + 10 = 30$).
There are **thirty**-three (33) students in my class.

# this

**1** *plural* **these**

"**This** is my sister's book. That is my book."
**2 This** week the weather is good. Last week it was very cold.
**3** "Listen to **this**! I'm going to America next week!"

# those

*plural of* **that**

"These pens cost fifteen pence. **Those** pens cost twenty-five pence."
"Are **those** your shoes?" – "Yes, they are."

# though

**1 Though** it was raining, Christopher did not use his umbrella.
**2** Maria saw her uncle in the street. She did not speak to him, **though**, because he was busy.

# thought

*verb*
**1** *past of* **think**
Peter **thought** for a moment. Then he answered the teacher's question.
*noun*
**2** *what you think*
No one knows what Kate thinks. She doesn't tell her **thoughts** to anyone.

# thousand

*the number* **1000**
A **thousand** people live in my village.
Six hundred plus eight hundred equals one **thousand** four hundred ($600 + 800 = 1400$).
There are **thousands of** fish in the lake.

# thread

Jenny is making a dress. She is using some **thread**.

thread

# three

*the number* **3**
Tom has **three** sisters.
Eleven minus eight equals **three** ($11 - 8 = 3$).

# threw

*past of* **throw**
Lisa **threw** the ball to her brother.

# through

*from one side to the other*
The students are going **through** the gate.
We walked **through** the market to the station.

# throw

**throwing, threw, thrown**

Kate is **throwing** the ball to Helen.

# thumb

thumb

*a part of the body*
A hand has four fingers and a **thumb**.

# thunder

*the loud noise that comes after lightning*
There was a storm last night. We saw some lightning. Then we heard the **thunder**.

# Thursday

Today is **Thursday**. Yesterday was Wednesday. Tomorrow will be Friday.
Susan sees her aunt on **Thursdays**.

# tick

*noun*
**1** This is a **tick**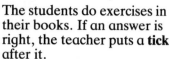
The students do exercises in their books. If an answer is right, the teacher puts a **tick** after it.
*verb*
**2** *to write a tick beside*
The students did an exercise and gave it to the teacher. The teacher **ticked** every answer that was right.

# ticket

Nick is at the station. He is buying a **ticket** for the train.

# tidy

**tidier, tidiest**
Kate's bedroom is **tidy**. She has put all her clothes and toys in cupboards.

# tie

tie

*noun*
**1** Peter is wearing a **tie**.

*verb* **tying, tied, tied**
**2** Kate **tied** some string around the box.

# tiger

*a large animal*
**Tigers** are yellow and black.
There are many **tigers** in India.

# tight

These shoes are too **tight**. They hurt my feet.

# till

*to a time*
Peter slept **till** ten o'clock this morning.
**Until** is another word for **till**.

# time

**1** "What's the **time**?" – "It's half past two."
**2** I worked for a long **time** yesterday.
**3** "I've read this book three **times**."
**4 on time**
*at the right time*
Helen came to school **on time** today, but Susan was late.

# times

Six **times** two is twelve (6 x 2 = 12).

# timetable

"What time does the train leave?" – "I don't know. Look at the **timetable**."

# tin

Alan is opening a **tin** of fruit.

# tinned

*in a tin or from a tin*
Alan had some **tinned** fruit for lunch.

# tiny

**tinier, tiniest**
*very small*
You can see some **tiny** fish in the river.

# tired

George has worked hard all day. Now he is very **tired**.

# to

1 Martin goes from London **to** Bristol by car.
2 Kate gave a present **to** her mother.
3 The train leaves at twenty **to** six (5.40).
4 Paul went to the zoo **to** see the animals.

# today

Yesterday was Tuesday. **Today** is Wednesday. Tomorrow will be Thursday.

Tom is at school **today**, but tomorrow he will have a holiday.

# toe

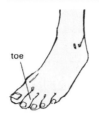

*a part of the foot*
We have ten **toes**.

# together

Nick walks to school with Tom. Nick and Tom walk to school **together**.

# toilet

There are two **toilets** at the station. One is for men, and the other is for women.
The **toilet** is in the bathroom.

# told

*past and part of* **tell**
"Sam has got a new job." – "How do you know?" – "He **told** me yesterday."

# tomato

*plural* **tomatoes**
*a red fruit*
Anne bought some **tomatoes** in the market.

# tomorrow

Today is Saturday. **Tomorrow** will be Sunday.
Steven will not go to work **tomorrow**.

# tongue

*a part of the mouth*
The doctor looked at Tom's **tongue**.

# tonight

*today at night*
I am going to the theatre **tonight**.

# too

1 David can drive a car. Martin can drive a car, **too**.
"I'm going to the shop." – "Can I come **too**?"
2 This box is **too** big. I can't carry it. The box is **too** big for me to carry.
"Did you go to the cinema?" – "No, there were **too** many people there."

# took

*past of* **take**
Uncle Christopher **took** me to school yesterday.

# tool

tools

*a thing that you use when you make something*
A shoemaker uses many **tools** for his work.

# tooth

*plural* **teeth**
*a part of the mouth*
**Teeth** are white. We use our **teeth** when we eat.

# toothache

Nick has eaten too many sweets. Now his tooth hurts. He has **toothache**.

# toothbrush

*plural* **toothbrushes**

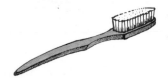

We clean our teeth with a **toothbrush**.

# toothpaste

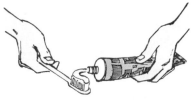

We use **toothpaste** to clean our teeth.

# top

**1** Susan is putting the **top** on the bottle.

**2** Helen is at the **top** of the stairs. Alan is at the bottom of the stairs.

**3 on top of**
The cat is sitting **on top of** the wall.

**4** *the highest*
"Where are the books?" – "In the **top** cupboard."

# torch

*plural* **torches**
*a small electric light that you can carry*
Helen cannot see anything in the dark cupboard. She needs a **torch**.

# tore

*past of the verb* **tear**
Peter **tore** his shirt when he was playing football.

# torn

*part of the verb* **tear**
"Look! You've **torn** your shirt, Peter!"

# total

Anne spent two pounds in the greengrocer's, six pounds in the grocer's and one pound in the baker's. The **total** was nine pounds (2 + 6 + 1 = 9).

# touch

*verb* **touches, touching, touched, touched**

**1** Susan **touched** Maria on the shoulder. "Hello, it's me!" she said.
*noun, plural* **touches**
**2** Maria felt a **touch** on her shoulder. It was her friend Susan.

# tourist

*a person who goes to another country for a holiday*
Many **tourists** visit America every year.

# towards

Jenny is walking **towards** the post office. Mark is walking away from it.

# towel

Peter is drying his hair with a **towel**.

# town

Bristol is a big **town**. A lot of people live there.

# toy

The children are playing with their **toys**. They have got a ball, a telephone, a train, and some cars.

# tractor

The farmer is driving a **tractor**.

# trade

*buying and selling*
There is a lot of **trade** between England and Spain.

# traffic

traffic lights

**1** *cars, buses, and lorries*
There is a lot of **traffic** in the town today.
**2 traffic lights**
The **traffic lights** are red. The cars must stop.

# train

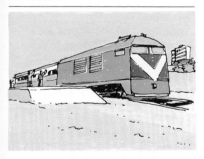

*noun*
**1** The **train** is leaving the railway station.

*verb*
**2** *to learn how to do something that is difficult*
David **trained** for five years to become a doctor.

# training

*learning how to do something that is difficult*
You must have many years of **training** if you want to be a lawyer.

# translate

*translating, translated, translated*
*to change something from one language into another language*
In the lesson, we **translated** a story from English into French.

# travel

**travelling, travelled, travelled**
*to go from one place to another place*
Christopher **travelled** from England to France by boat.

# traveller

*a person who is going from one place to another place*
There are a lot of **travellers** on the roads to London today.

# tray

The waiter is carrying some food on a **tray**.

tray

# treasure

*gold, silver, and things that cost a lot of money*
There was a lot of **treasure** in the pyramids.

# tree

There are some **trees** near the river.

# triangle

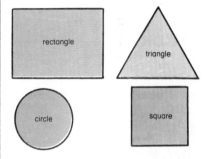

rectangle

triangle

circle

square

A **triangle** has three sides.

# trick

**1** *something you do that is clever*
The elephants in the circus did some **tricks** with balls.
**2** *something you do as a joke*
Paul played a **trick** on his brother. He put salt in the sugar bowl, so that his brother put salt into his coffee.

# tried

*past and part of* **try**
I **tried** to open the door, but it was locked.

# trip

*going to a place for a short time*
Peter and Tom went on a **trip** to the sea yesterday. They left home early in the morning and came back late at night.

# trouble

**1** *a problem*
"I'm sorry we're late. We had some **trouble** with our car."
**2 in trouble**
That man is **in trouble** with the police. He has done something bad.

# trousers

Nick is wearing a new pair of **trousers**.

# truck

*a lorry*
Robert drives a **truck**. His **truck** can carry a lot of things.

# true

**truer, truest**
"Susan says that she can speak French. Is that **true**?" – "Yes. Her father taught her."

# truth

"Susan says she can speak French. Is that true?" – "Yes, she is telling the **truth**. She can speak French."

# try

**tries, trying, tried, tried**

**1** Tom is **trying** to lift the box, but he can't. The box is too heavy.

**2 to try on**
Helen needed some new shoes. She **tried** some shoes **on** in the shoeshop. They were the right size, so she bought them.

# T-shirt

Michael is wearing a **T-shirt**.

# tube

Nick is using a **tube** of toothpaste.

# Tuesday

Today is **Tuesday**. Yesterday was Monday. Tomorrow will be Wednesday.
On **Tuesdays** Helen has an English lesson.

# turn

*verb*
**1** "Where is the hospital?" – "Go along this street and **turn** left at the end."
Helen **turned round** when her brother came into the room.
**2** When a car moves, its wheels **turn**.
**3** *to become*
This plant has no water. The leaves are **turning** brown.
**4 to turn into**
*to become something else*
Water **turns into** ice when it is very cold.
**5 to turn on**
"It is very dark in this room. Please **turn** the light **on**."
Nick **turned on** the tap and filled the bottle with water.
**6 to turn off**
Robert **turned off** the radio when he went out of the room.
*noun*
**7** "You've been playing with that toy all day. It's my **turn** to play with it now."

# turning

"How can I get to the post office?" – "Go along this street and take the first **turning** on the right."

# TV

*television*
Peter watches **TV** in the evening.

# twelfth

December is the **twelfth** month of the year.
Today's date is the **twelfth** of August (**12th** August).

# twelve

*the number* 12
There are **twelve** months in a year.
Eight plus four equals **twelve** (8 + 4 = **12**).

# twenty

*the number* 20
There are **twenty** students in our class.
Eight plus twelve equals **twenty** (8 + 12 = **20**).
My brother is **twenty**-five (25) years old.

# twice

*two times*
Anne goes to the shops on Mondays and Wednesdays. She goes to the shops **twice** a week.

# two

*the number* **2**
Lisa has **two** brothers.
One plus one equals **two** (1 + 1 = **2**).

# tying

*part of* **tie**

Jenny is **tying** her dog to a tree. She is going into a shop.

# type

*verb* **typing, typed, typed**

**1** Elaine is **typing** a letter.
*noun*
**2** "What is a parrot?" – "It's a **type** of bird."

# typewriter

*a machine for typing*
Elaine has an electric **typewriter** in her office.

# tyre

tyre

Peter is putting a new **tyre** on his bicycle.

# U u

## ugly

**uglier, ugliest**
*not beautiful*
"Do you like that picture?" – "No, I think it's **ugly**."

## umbrella

It is raining, but Christopher has an **umbrella**.

## uncle

*the brother of your mother or your father*
**Uncle** Steven is my mother's brother.

## under

**1** The cat is **under** the chair.

**2** *less than*
All the students in our school are **under** sixteen years old.

## underground

*a railway under the ground in some big cities*
When Christopher is in London, he travels on the **underground**.

## underneath

**1** *under*
Helen's book is **underneath** Alan's book.

**2** *below*
When Peter draws a picture, he writes his name **underneath**.

## understand

**understanding, understood, understood**

Tom cannot **understand** what he is reading.

## undress

**undresses, undressing, undressed, undressed**
*to take your clothes off*
Paul **undresses** before he goes to bed at night.

## unfortunately

Martin wants to buy a car, but **unfortunately** he has not got enough money.

## uniform

Nurses wear a **uniform** when they are working. Policemen and soldiers wear **uniforms**, too.

## university

*plural* **universities**
*a place where people study after they leave school*
Susan's sister is studying English at Bristol **University**.

## unless

"Lisa, you will be late for school **unless** you go now." – "Yes, mother. I'm going."

## until

*to a time*
Our teacher told us to read **until** the end of the lesson.
**Till** is another word for **until**.

## up

**1** *not down*
Helen is walking **up** the stairs. Alan is walking down the stairs.

Paul threw the ball **up** in the air.
**2** *out of bed in the morning*
"Is Tom **up**?" – "No, he's still in bed."

## upside down

The glasses are **upside down**.

## upstairs

Our house has two floors. We sleep **upstairs** and we eat downstairs.
"Go **upstairs** and get your blue shirt, Peter." – "Yes, mother."

## us

We opened our books when the teacher told **us** to open them.
"We're going to the cinema, Paul. Do you want to come with **us**?"

## use

**using, used, used**
"Can I **use** your telephone, please?" – "Yes, of course."
Nick **used** five oranges to make a glass of orange juice.

## used to

**1** I **used to** walk to school every day, but now I go to school by bus.
We **used to** live in Bristol. We came to London last year.
**2 to be used to**
"It's very noisy in your office, Christopher." – "I **am used to** it. It doesn't worry me."

## useful

*that helps you to do something*
My new bicycle is very **useful**. I go to school on it, I use it to go to the town, and I can go to my friend's house on it.

## usual

"When did you have lunch today?" – "At two o'clock, **as usual**."

## usually

Peter **usually** gets up at seven o'clock, but yesterday he got up at nine o'clock because it was a school holiday.

# V v

## valley

*low ground between hills*
You can see a river in this **valley**.

## van

Robert is driving a **van**.

## vase

*something that you put flowers in*
Maria is putting some water in the **vase**.

vase

## vegetable

*part of a plant that you can eat*
Onions and potatoes are **vegetables**. Bananas and oranges are fruit.

## verb

*a word that tells us what a person or a thing does*
"Go", "put", and "run" are **verbs**.

# verse

*a part of a poem or a song*
This song has twenty lines. It has four **verses**. There are five lines in each **verse**.

# very

**1** Horses are big animals. Elephants are **very** big animals.
Egypt is a **very** hot country.
That old man walks **very** slowly.
**2 very well**
"How are you?" – "I'm **very well**, thank you."
**3 very much**
"Do you like football?" – "Yes. I like it **very much**."
"Here is a present for you." – "Thank you **very much**."

# view

*what you can see from a place*
There is a good **view** of the sea from my hotel.

# village

*a small town*
Two hundred people live in this **village**.

# visa

**1** *something in your passport that says you can go to a country*
You must have a **visa** when you go to America.
**2** In some countries, you must have an **exit visa** when you want to leave the country.

# visit

*verb*
**1** Helen's uncle and aunt live in France. She **visits** them every summer.
*noun*
**2** Tom is in hospital. He had a **visit** from his friends yesterday.

# visitor

*someone who goes to see a person or a place*
Tom had a lot of **visitors** when he was in hospital.
The British Museum has many **visitors** every year.

# voice

Everyone can hear Alan when he speaks. He has a very loud **voice**.

# volleyball

*a game for two teams that you play with a ball*
These boys are playing **volleyball**.

# vowel

These English letters are called **vowels: a, e, i, o, u**. The other letters are called consonants.

# voyage

David went to America by ship. The **voyage** took five days.

# Ww

# wait

Some people are **waiting** at the railway station. They are **waiting for** a train.

# waiter

Nick and Tom are in a cafe. The **waiter** is bringing them some food.

# wake up

**waking up, woke up, woken up**
Alan slept for eight hours. Then he **woke up**.

# walk

*verb*
**1** Peter is on his bicycle. Michael is **walking** beside him.
*noun*
**2** We went for a **walk** near the river yesterday.

# wall

There is a **wall** round the garden. The dog cannot get out.

# wallet

Men keep their money in a **wallet**.

# want

"Do you **want** a drink, Peter?" – "Yes, some coffee, please, mother."
"I **want** to go to England next summer." – "You'll need a ticket, and an umbrella!"

# war

The Second World **War** was from 1939 to 1945.

# warm

*not cool, but not very hot*
The weather is **warm** today.

# warn

*to tell someone that there is danger*
The teacher **warned** the children that the railway was dangerous. She **warned** them **not to** play near the railway.

# was

*past of* **be**
Today is Wednesday. Yesterday **was** Tuesday.
"Were you at school yesterday?" – "Yes, I **was**."

# wash

**washes, washing, washed, washed**

**1** Nick is **washing** his hands.

washbasin

**2 to wash up**
*to clean the plates with water after a meal*
"Can you **wash up**, please, Lisa?" – "Yes, of course, mother."

# washbasin

Nick is washing his hands in a **washbasin**.

# wasn't

*was not*
"Was Peter at school today?" – "No, he **wasn't**."

# watch

*verb* **watches, watching, watched, watched**

**1** Louise is **watching** the children playing.
**2 to watch television**
Peter **watches television** every night.

*noun, plural* **watches**
**3** Kate is looking at her **watch**.

# water

*noun*
**1** Nick is putting some **water** in the jug.

*verb*
**2** *to put water on plants*
In the summer, we **water** the plants outside our house every day.

# watermelon

*a round fruit*
We can buy **watermelons** in the market.

# wave

*verb* **waving, waved, waved**

**1** Elaine is **waving** to the children.
*noun*
**2** *water moving up and down*
The wind is very strong. There are a lot of **waves** on the sea.

# way

**1** "Can you tell me the **way** to the station, please?" – "Go along this street and turn left."
Peter walked to school. **On the way** he saw his friend Tom.
**2** "Is the post office near here?" – "No, it's a long **way** from here."
**3** *how you do something*
"Do you know the **way** to cook this vegetable?"
"TV" is a short **way** of saying "television".

## we

My brother and I are going to London tomorrow. **We** are going to visit some friends.

## wear

**wearing, wore, worn**
Susan is **wearing** a scarf. Her sister is not **wearing** a scarf.

Tom puts on his school clothes every morning. He must **wear** them at school.

## weather

Yesterday the **weather** was very bad. There was a lot of rain. Today, it is hot and sunny.

## we'd

**1** *we would*
"**We'd** like to come to the cinema with you, but we must do some work."
**2** *we had*
The lesson ended before **we'd** finished our work.

## wedding

Martin and Isabel got married yesterday. Lots of people came to their **wedding**.

# Wednesday

Today is **Wednesday**. Yesterday was Tuesday. Tomorrow will be Thursday. Anne goes to the shops on **Wednesdays**.

## weed

*a plant that grows where you do not want it*
Mark pulled the **weeds** out of his garden.

## week

There are seven days in the **week**: Sunday, Monday, Tuesday, Wednesday, Thursday, Friday, and Saturday.

## weekend

*Saturday and Sunday*
This **weekend**, Jenny is going to visit her uncle.

## weigh

**1** "How much do these oranges **weigh**?" – "They **weigh** one kilo."

**2** The shopkeeper **weighed** some oranges.

## weight

"What is the **weight** of these oranges?" – "They weigh one kilo."

## welcome

**1** Peter visited his friend John in London. "**Welcome** to London," said John.
**2** "**You're welcome.**"
"I've repaired your kite." – "Thank you very much." – "**You're welcome.**"

## we'll

*we will*
"**We'll** carry those boxes for you, mother." – "Thank you."

## well

**1** Susan is a good student. She can speak French very **well**.
**2** Tom is not **well**. The doctor came to see him today.
**3 as well**
*also*
Anne bought some oranges in the market. She bought a melon **as well**. She bought a melon **as well as** some oranges.

*noun*
**4** This old man is getting some water from a **well**.

## went

*past of* **go**
"Where did you go yesterday?" – "I **went** to the zoo."

## we're

*we are*
"Alan and I go to the same school. **We're** in the same class."

## were

*past of* **be**
"Where **were** Peter and Nick yesterday?" – "They **were** at school."

## weren't

*were not*
"I went to see Peter and Lisa, but they **weren't** at home."
"Why **weren't** you at school yesterday, Tom?" – "I was ill."

## west

*noun*
**1** In the evening, the sun goes down in the **west**.
*adjective*
**2** Nigeria is in **West** Africa.

Bristol is **west of** London.

# western

Bordeaux is in **western** France. Manchester is in the **western** part of England.

# wet

**wetter, wettest**
Tom fell into the water. Now his clothes are **wet**.

# we've

*we have*
**We've** got a new car. It goes very fast.

# whale

*a very large animal*
**Whales** live in the sea.

# what

1 "**What** did you buy?" – "I bought a newspaper."
2 In the lesson, the teacher tells us **what** to do.
3 "**What** a hot day it is!"
4 "**What for?**"
"*Why?*"
"I'm going to the post office."
– "**What for?**" – "I need some stamps."

# wheat

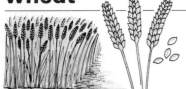

We make bread from **wheat**.

# wheel

A bicycle has two **wheels**. Cars have four **wheels**.

# when

1 "**When** does the next lesson start?" – "At ten o'clock."
2 I lived in a village **when** I was young.

# where

1 "**Where** are the plates?" – "They are in the cupboard."
2 That is the house **where** I live.

# whether

*if*
I don't know **whether** there are any snakes in England.

# which

1 "**Which** pen is yours, the blue pen or the red pen?" – "The blue pen."
2 This is the book **which** Helen gave me.

# while

1 Peter watched television **while** he ate his dinner.
2 *some time*
Martin waited at the station. After **a while**, the train came.

# whisper

*to speak very quietly*
Kate **whispered** to her friend. She did not want the teacher to hear her.

# whistle

*noun*
1 The teacher blew a **whistle** to start the race.

*verb* **whistling, whistled, whistled**
2 *to make a noise like a whistle*
Mark **whistled** to his dog, and the dog came to him.

# white

*the colour of milk*
*noun*
1 **White** is a good colour to wear in hot countries.
*adjective* **whiter, whitest**
2 My grandfather has **white** hair.

# who

1 "**Who** is that man?" – "That's Andrew, the grocer."
2 Sam is the shoemaker **who** works in that shop.

# whole

*all of something*
I ate the **whole** bag of sweets.

# whom

That is the boy to **whom** I gave the kite.

# who's

*who is*
"**Who's** that?" – "That's my friend Tom."

# whose

1 "**Whose** book is this?" – "It's Maria's book."
2 "Who is that?" – "That is the woman **whose** son lives in America."

# why

1 "**Why** are you running?" – "Because I'm late for school."
2 I don't know **why** David is not here.
3 "**Why not?**"
"I'm not going to school today." – "**Why not?**" – "Because I'm ill."

# wide

**wider, widest**
**1** The river is very **wide**. I cannot swim across it.

**2** "How **wide** is that table?" – "It's one metre **wide** and two metres long."

# wife

*plural* **wives**
David and Janet are married. Janet is David's **wife**. David is Janet's husband.

# wild

In Africa there are many **wild** animals, such as lions and elephants.

# will

Next year James **will** be eighteen. He **will** leave school and start work.

# win

**winning, won, won**

*to do best in a game*
Nick and Tom had a race. Nick **won** the race. Tom lost the race.

# wind

There is a lot of **wind** today. This man is holding on to his hat.

# window

Kate is opening the **window**.

# windy

**windier, windiest**
There is a lot of wind today. It is very **windy**.

# wing

wing
wing

A bird has two **wings**. A plane has **wings**, too.

# winner

*a person who does best in a game*
Tom and Nick had a race. Nick ran faster than Tom. Nick was the **winner**.

# winter

*a part of the year*
**Winter** comes after autumn. It is colder than autumn.
In England, it sometimes snows in the **winter**.

# wire

*a long thin piece of metal*
There are some telephone **wires** next to the road.

# wise

**wiser, wisest**
*knowing and understanding many things*
My grandfather is a **wise** old man. He can always answer my questions.

# wish

*verb* **wishes, wishing, wished, wished**
**1** *to want something that you cannot have*
I **wish** that I could visit my brother in America.
**2** *to want*
"I **wish** to see the headmaster, please," said Peter's mother.
*noun, plural* **wishes**
**3** Best wishes
Helen wrote a letter to her friend. At the end of the letter she wrote: "**Best wishes**, Helen".

# with

**1** Peter walks to school **with** his brother.
**2** Kate writes **with** a pencil.
**3** *having*
"Who is that man **with** the moustache?" – "That's my Uncle Steven."

# without

**1** You cannot buy things **without** money.
**2** "Can you carry these eggs **without** breaking them, Paul?"

## wives

*plural of* **wife**
"Who are those two ladies?" –
"They are the **wives** of David
and Steven."

## woke up

*past of* **wake up**
Kate **woke up** early this
morning.

## woken up

*part of* **wake up**
"Where's Peter?" – "He's
asleep. He hasn't **woken up**
yet."

## wolf

*plural* **wolves**

*an animal like a big dog*
These are **wolves**.

## woman

*plural* **women**
Jane is a
**woman**.
Steven is a
man.

## won

*past and part of* **win**
Susan is very good at French.
Last year she **won** a prize for
French at school.

## wonder

*to ask yourself*
I **wonder** what time it is.

## wonderful

*very good*
"Did you have a good
holiday?" – "Yes, we had a
**wonderful** time."

## won't

*will not*
"I **won't** play football today,
because it's raining."

## wood

**1** *what trees are made of*
Martin made a table from
some pieces of **wood**.
**2** *a small forest*
I went for a walk in the **wood**.

## wool

We get **wool** from sheep. We
can make clothes from **wool**.

## woollen

*made of wool*
Kate has a **woollen** dress.

## word

"House" is the **word** for the
place where we live. The
French **word** for "house" is
"maison".

## wore

*past of* **wear**
Nick **wore** his new trousers
yesterday.

## work

*verb*
**1** William is a teacher. He
**works** in a school in London.
**2** Our television is not **working**.
A man is coming to repair it
tomorrow.

*noun*
**3** Elaine is a secretary. She
goes to **work** at nine o'clock.

## workman

*plural* **workmen**

*a man who works with his
hands*
The **workmen** are making a
new road.

## world

*all the countries and all the
people*
The Nile is the longest river in
the **world**.

## worn

*part of* **wear**
"Have you **worn** your new
trousers yet?" – "Yes, I wore
them yesterday."

## worried

*adjective*
**1** *thinking that something is not
all right*
Nick went to the shops with his
young sister, but now he
cannot find her. He is very
**worried**.
*verb*
**2** *past and part of* **worry**
I **worried** about my uncle when
he was in hospital.

## worry

**worries, worrying, worried,
worried**
*to be afraid and think that
something is not all right*
Susan's mother and father
**worry** if Susan is late home.

## worse

Yesterday the weather was bad, but today it is very bad. It is **worse** than yesterday.

## worst

"Did you like the film?" – "No! It was the **worst** film I've ever seen!"

## worth

"How much is that bicycle?" – "Fifty pounds." – "But it isn't **worth** fifty pounds! I'll give you thirty pounds for it."

## would

**1** *past of* **will**
Helen said that she **would** come and see me today.
**2** If I had a lot of money, I **would** buy a new car.
**3** "**Would** you help me, please?" – "Yes, of course."
**4 would like**
"**Would** you **like** some tea?" – "Yes, please."
Lisa **would like** to go to see her aunt this summer.

## wouldn't

*would not*
"If I had a lot of money, I **wouldn't** go to work."

## wrap

**wrapping, wrapped, wrapped**

Jenny is **wrapping** a book in paper. It is a present for Kate.

## wrist

*a part of the body*

Peter wears a watch on his **wrist**.

## write

**writing, wrote, written**

**1** Susan is **writing**.
**2 to write to**
*to write and send a letter*
Kate often **writes to** her aunt.

## writer

*a person who writes books*
Charles Dickens was a **writer**. Many people read his books.
**Author** is another word for **writer**.

## writing

| Lisa | Helen |
|---|---|

Lisa's **writing** is very good.
Helen's **writing** is bad.

## written

*part of* **write**
Kate has **written** a lot of letters today.

## wrong

**1** "Two and two are five." – "No, that's **wrong**!" – "Two and two are four." – "Yes, that's right."
**2** It is **wrong** to talk when the teacher is talking.

## wrote

*past of* **write**
Susan **wrote** a letter to her brother yesterday.

# X x

# Y y

## yard

This little boy is riding his bicycle in the **yard** of his house.

## year

There are 365 days in a **year**. Kate is fifteen **years** old. Her sister is thirteen.

## yellow

*the colour of the middle of an egg*
*noun*
**1 Yellow** is my favourite colour.
*adjective*
**2** Kate has a **yellow** dress.

## yes

"Is Venice in Italy?" – "**Yes**, it is."

## yesterday

**Yesterday** was Friday. Today is Saturday. Tomorrow will be Sunday.

Aunt Jane came to see us **yesterday**.

## yet

**1** "Have you done that work **yet**?" – "No, I'm still doing it."
**2 not yet**
"Christopher is coming back from America today." – "Has he telephoned?" – "No, **not yet**."

## you

**1** "I can swim. Can **you** swim too, Peter?" – "Yes, I can."

"Where are **you**, Maria?" – "I'm here, in the kitchen."

"I'm going to the shops." – "I'll come with **you**."

**2** "Did **you** all go to the cinema yesterday?" – "Yes, we did."

"Tom and Nick – did Alan give those books to **you**?" – "Yes, he did."

**3** *any person*
**You** can see lions in the zoo.

## you'd

**1** *you would*
"You said that **you'd** help me, but you didn't do anything."
**2** *you had*
"We came to see you in the cafe, but **you'd** gone."

## you'll

*you will*
"I think **you'll** like the new student. She's very nice."

## young

*not old*
David's children are very **young**. They do not go to school.

Those **young** trees need a lot of water.

## your

"Is that my book?" – "No, it's Helen's. **Your** book is on the desk."

## you're

*you are*
"Peter is a good swimmer. **You're** a good swimmer too, Michael."

## yours

"This is my book. **Yours** is on the desk."

## yourself

*plural* **yourselves**
**1** "You've cut **yourself**, Alan." – "Yes. I fell off my bicycle this morning."
**2** *without any help*
"Did you make this table **yourself**?" – "Yes. Nobody helped me."
**3 by yourself**
*without any other person*
"You must go to school **by yourself** today, Paul," said his father.

## yourselves

*plural of* **yourself**
"Did you enjoy **yourselves** at the cinema?" – "Yes, we did."

## you've

*you have*
"**You've** got a lot of books, Alan."

# Z z

## zebra

*an animal like a horse*
A **zebra** is black and white.

## zero

*the number* **0**
The man said, "Three ... two ... one ... **zero**!" The rocket left the Earth.

## zoo

*a place where you can see many different animals*
We saw a lion and some elephants at the **zoo**.